CLIFFS

Preliminary Scholastic Aptitude Test
and
National Merit Scholarship
Qualifying Test (NMSQT)

PREPARATION GUIDE

by

Jerry Bobrow, Ph.D.

and

William A. Covino, Ph.D.

Contributing Authors

Bernard V. Zandy, M.S.
Bill Bobrow, M.A.

Consultants

Peter Z. Orton, M.Ed.
Merritt L. Weisinger, J.D.
David A. Kay, M.S.

D1212213

LINCOLN, NEBRASKA   68501

ACKNOWLEDGMENTS

I would like to thank the following people for their invaluable assistance in typing, proofreading, and editing the manuscript: my wife, Susan Bobrow; my coordinating assistant, Joy Mondragon, and my typist, Sally Reilly. I also wish to thank Harry Kaste of Cliffs Notes for his vigilant final editing and uncompromising attention to every detail of the production process.

Thanks are also extended to Dr. Albert Upton for allowing me to use excerpts from his book Design for Thinking.

CONTENTS

PART III: PRACTICE-REVIEW-ANALYZE

PREFACE

YOUR PSAT/NMSQT SCORES ARE IMPORTANT! They can help you (1) plan your college career, (2) get a scholarship, and (3) practice for the SAT for college entrance. Therefore, your study time must be used most effectively. You need the most comprehensive test preparation guide that you can realistically complete in a reasonable time. It must be short, direct, precise, easy-to-use, and thorough, giving you all the information you need to do your best on the PSAT/NMSQT.

In keeping with the fine tradition of Cliffs Notes, this guide was developed by leading experts in the field of test preparation as part of a series to specifically meet these standards. The testing strategies, techniques, and materials have been researched, tested, and evaluated, and are presently used at test preparation programs at many leading colleges and universities. This guide emphasizes the BOBROW TEST PREPARATION SERVICES approach, which focuses on six major areas:

1. Ability Tested
2. Basic Skills Necessary
3. Understanding Directions
4. Analysis of Directions
5. Suggested Approaches with Samples
6. Practice-Review-Analyze

These major areas include important mathematical terminology, formulas, and a helpful list of prefixes, suffixes, and roots, followed by a complete practice exam with answers and in-depth explanations.

This guide was written to give you the edge in doing your best by giving you maximum benefit in a reasonable amount of time and is meant to augment, not substitute for, formal or informal learning throughout junior high and high school. If you follow the Study Guide Checklist in this book and study regularly, you will get the best test preparation possible.

STUDY GUIDE CHECKLIST

_____ 1. Read the PSAT/NMSQT Information Bulletin.

_____ 2. Become familiar with the Test Format, page 3.

_____ 3. Familiarize yourself with the answers to Questions Commonly Asked about the PSAT, page 5.

_____ 4. Learn the techniques of Two Successful Overall Approaches, page 7.

_____ 5. Carefully read Part II, Analysis of Exam Areas, beginning on page 11.

_____ 6. Review lists of Common Prefixes, Suffixes, and Roots, page 20.

_____ 7. Review math Terminology, Formulas, and General Information, page 34.

_____ 8. Strictly observing time allotments, take the Full-Length Practice Test, section-by-section, beginning on page 47.

_____ 9. Check your answers and make corrections, page 72.

_____ 10. Analyze your Practice Test results, page 73.

_____ 11. Fill out the Tally Sheet for Problems Missed to pinpoint your mistakes, page 75.

_____ 12. While referring to each item of the Practice Test, study ALL the Answers and Explanations that begin on page 79.

_____ 13. Review as necessary Basic Skills, Terminology, Formulas, and General Information given in Part II of this book.

_____ 14. CAREFULLY READ "FINAL PREPARATION" on page 99.

PART I: Introduction

COMMON FORMAT OF A RECENT PSAT/NMSQT EXAM

Section I	Verbal Ability	65 Questions
50 Minutes	Antonyms	12–18 Questions
	Analogies	12–18 Questions
	Sentence Completion	12–18 Questions
	Reading Comprehension	18–25 Questions

Section II	Mathematical Ability	50 Questions
50 Minutes	Math Ability	32–40 Questions
	Quantitative Comparison	10–18 Questions

Total Testing Time 100 Minutes = 1 Hour, 40 Minutes	Approximately 115 Questions

GENERAL DESCRIPTION

The PSAT/NMSQT measures verbal and mathematical abilities related to college. It is a preview of the SAT (Scholastic Aptitude Test), which is usually required for admission to college. The results of the test should help you plan your college career. The test lasts one hour and forty minutes, and consists entirely of multiple-choice questions.

You will spend 50 minutes on a verbal section (65 questions) and 50 minutes on a mathematical section (50 questions). The verbal section tests your reading comprehension and the breadth of your vocabulary. The math section presents problems in arithmetic, algebra, and geometry.

QUESTIONS COMMONLY ASKED ABOUT THE PSAT/NMSQT

Q: WHO ADMINISTERS THE PSAT/NMSQT?
A: The PSAT/NMSQT is administered by the College Entrance Examination Board and the National Merit Scholarship Corporation in conjunction with Educational Testing Service of Princeton, New Jersey.

Q: WHAT IS THE DIFFERENCE BETWEEN THE PSAT AND THE NMSQT?
A: Taking the PSAT (Preliminary Scholastic Aptitude Test) qualifies you to compete in the National Merit Scholarship Program. So another name for the PSAT is the NMSQT (National Merit Scholarship Qualifying Test).

Q: CAN I TAKE THE PSAT/NMSQT MORE THAN ONCE?
A: You may take the test only once in a school year. The PSAT/NMSQT is administered once a year, in October. Your high school will inform you of the test date and invite you and your fellow students to take the test.

Q: WHAT MATERIALS MAY I BRING TO THE PSAT/NMSQT?
A: Bring your registration form, positive identification, a watch, three or four sharpened Number 2 pencils, and a good eraser. You may not bring scratchpaper, calculators, or books. You may do your figuring in the margins of the test booklet or in the space provided.

Q: MAY I CANCEL MY SCORE?
A: Yes. You may do so by notifying your test supervisor *before* you leave the examination room.

Q: SHOULD I GUESS ON THE PSAT/NMSQT?
A: If you can eliminate one or more of the multiple-choice answers to a question, it is to your advantage to guess. Eliminating one or more answers increases your chance of choosing the right answer. To discourage wild guessing, a fraction of a point is subtracted for every wrong answer, but no points are subtracted if you leave the answer blank.

Q: HOW SHOULD I PREPARE FOR THE PSAT/NMSQT?
A: Understanding and practicing test-taking strategies will help a great deal, especially on the verbal section. Subject-matter review is particularly useful for the math section. Subject matter and strategies are covered in this book.

Q: HOW AND WHEN SHOULD I REGISTER?
A: After your school notifies you of the time and place of testing, report to that location on the test day to register and pay the required fee.

Q: WHAT ARE THE NMSC SCHOLARSHIPS?
A: The National Merit Scholarship Corporation awards scholarships to about 4000 winners each year; it also sponsors an achievement program which tries to increase educational opportunities for minority students. Further information about the merit and achievement programs is available in the official PSAT/NMSQT Bulletin.

Q: HOW DO I OBTAIN A BULLETIN AND FURTHER INFORMATION ABOUT THE PSAT/NMSQT?
A: Check with your high school counselor or write to the following agencies:

1. To get information about the test itself, write to

> PSAT/NMSQT
> Box 1025
> Berkeley, California 94701
> (415) 849-0950

If you live in Mexico, western Canada, Alaska, Arizona, Arkansas, California, Colorado, Hawaii, Idaho, Montana, Nevada, New Mexico, Oklahoma, Oregon, Texas, Utah, Washington, or Wyoming.

2. If you live in any other state or in eastern Canada, write to

> PSAT/NMSQT
> Box 589
> Princeton, New Jersey 08540
> (609) 921-9000

3. To get information about NMSC scholarship programs, write to

> National Merit Scholarship Corporation
> Educational Services Department
> One American Plaza
> Evanston, Illinois 60201
> (312) 866-5100

TAKING THE PSAT/NMSQT: TWO SUCCESSFUL OVERALL APPROACHES

I. The "Plus-Minus" System

Many who take the PSAT/NMSQT don't get their best possible score because they spend too much time on difficult questions, leaving insufficient time to answer the easy questions. Don't let this happen to you. Since every question within each section is worth the same amount, use the following system, *marking on your answer sheet:*

1. Answer easy questions immediately.
2. Place a "+" next to any problem that seems solvable but is too time-consuming.
3. Place a "−" next to any problem that seems impossible. Act quickly; don't waste time deciding whether a problem is a "+" or a "−".

After working all the problems you can do immediately, go back and work your "+" problems. If you finish them, try your "−" problems (sometimes when you come back to a problem that seemed impossible you will suddenly realize how to solve it).

Your answer sheet should look something like this after you finish working your easy questions:

$$
\begin{array}{lll}
& 1. & Ⓐ\ ● \ Ⓒ\ Ⓓ\ Ⓔ \\
+ & 2. & Ⓐ\ Ⓑ\ Ⓒ\ Ⓓ\ Ⓔ \\
& 3. & Ⓐ\ Ⓑ\ ●\ Ⓓ\ Ⓔ \\
- & 4. & Ⓐ\ Ⓑ\ Ⓒ\ Ⓓ\ Ⓔ \\
+ & 5. & Ⓐ\ Ⓑ\ Ⓒ\ Ⓓ\ Ⓔ
\end{array}
$$

Make sure to erase your "+" and "−" marks before your time is up. The scoring machine may count extraneous marks as wrong answers.

II. The Elimination Strategy

Take advantage of being allowed to mark in your testing booklet. As you eliminate an answer choice from consideration, *make sure to mark it out in your question booklet* as follows:

? (A̶)
  (B)
  (C̶)
  (D̶)
? (E)

7

Notice that some choices are marked with question marks, signifying that they may be possible answers. This technique will help you avoid reconsidering those choices you have already eliminated and will help you narrow down your possible answers.

These marks in your testing booklet do not need to be erased.

PART II: Analysis of Exam Areas

This section is designed to introduce you to each PSAT/NMSQT area by carefully reviewing the—

1. Ability Tested
2. Basic Skills Necessary
3. Directions
4. Analysis of Directions
5. Suggested Approach with Sample Problems

This section emphasizes important test-taking techniques and strategies and how to apply them to a variety of problem types. It also includes valuable terminology, formulas, basic math information, and a compact list of prefixes, suffixes, and roots to assist you in the verbal section.

INTRODUCTION TO VERBAL ABILITY

The Verbal Ability sections of the PSAT/NMSQT consist of four types of questions; antonyms and analogies, sentence completion, and reading comprehension. The section is 50 minutes in length and contains 60 to 65 questions. This section generates a scaled Verbal Ability score that ranges from 20 to 80, with an average score of about 43 for Juniors later entering college.

A CAREFUL ANALYSIS OF EACH TYPE OF VERBAL ABILITY QUESTION FOLLOWS.

ANTONYMS

Ability Tested

The Antonym section tests your vocabulary—your ability to understand the meanings of words and to distinguish between fine shades of meaning.

Basic Skills Necessary

This section requires a strong high school vocabulary. A strong vocabulary cannot be developed instantly: it grows over a long period of time spent reading widely and learning new words. Knowing the meanings of prefixes, suffixes, and roots will help you to derive word meanings on the test.

Directions

Each word in CAPITAL LETTERS is followed by five words or phrases. The correct choice is the word or phrase whose meaning is most nearly *opposite* to the meaning of the word in capitals. You may be required to distinguish fine shades of meaning. Look at all choices before marking your answer.

Analysis

1. Although your choice may not be a "perfect" opposite, it must be the *most nearly opposite* of the five choices provided.

2. You should consider all the choices, keeping in mind that in most cases *three* of the five choices can be quickly eliminated as not at all opposite to the original word.

Suggested Approach With Samples

1. The prefix, root, and (sometimes suffix of the original word may help you locate its opposite. *Example:*

PROVOCATIVE
(A) persistent   (C) final   (E) certain
(B) liberal   (D) inconsequential

The prefix *pro-* has several meanings, and all of them have "positive" connotations; here it means "forth" or "forward." Of the five choices, the prefix most opposite to the meaning of *pro-* is *in-*: the connotations of *in-* are often negative; here it means "not."

Our suspicion that these words are opposite is further supported by considering their roots. The root word of *provocative* is the Latin term *vocare,* which means "to call." Therefore, *provocative* is associated with "calling forth." The root word of *inconsequential* is "consequence." Therefore, *inconsequential* means "of no consequence" or "unimportant" and is the most nearly opposite to something that excites or provokes. (D) is the best choice.

2. Without considering the parts of the original word, you may be able to detect whether it is "positive" or "negative" in meaning. If the original word is positive, your choice must be negative, and vice versa. *Example:*

GHASTLY
(A) crazy   (C) fine   (E) plain
(B) lonesome   (D) handsome

Ghastly is a strongly negative word. Although *fine* is a positive word, and therefore opposite to *ghastly, handsome* is a positive word specifically related to appearance and is therefore most nearly opposite to *ghastly,* which denotes a frightful appearance.

3. Working from the answer choices and looking for a single choice that "stands out" can be a useful strategy. *Example:*

TRANSGRESS
(A) disappoint   (C) obey   (E) devastate
(B) disturb   (D) pollute

Assessing the choices for "positive" or "negative" meaning, notice that only *obey* is not a negative word; thus, it "stands out" among the other choices. In this case, *obey* is the opposite of *transgress,* which means "to break a law."

4. Don't choose an antonym that is too broad or too limited to be an opposite.

LACONIC

(A) long   (C) lavish   (E) many-sided
(B) talkative   (D) liberal

Laconic means "using few words." Although (A), (C), (D), and (E) are all partial opposites because they contain the idea of "much" as opposed to "few," only (B) specifically refers to language.

5. Try using the given word in a short, clear sentence; try to think of how you've heard the word used before. You may discover a context for it that will help you make a choice. *Example:*

CATASTROPHIC

(A) luck   (C) successful   (E) manageable
(B) accident   (D) disastrous

Sentence: "Losing my wallet was catastrophic" (the cause of a sudden, great disaster). Since a catastrophic experience is something negative, the correct choice is positive (C).

ANALOGIES

Ability Tested

The Analogy section tests your ability to understand logical relationships between pairs of words. Your vocabulary—your ability to understand the meanings of words—is also tested.

Basic Skills Necessary

The basic skills necessary for this section are, once again, a strong high school vocabulary and the ability to distinguish similarities and differences between words or ideas.

Directions

In each following sample, you are given a related pair of words or phrases. Select the lettered pair that *best* expresses a relationship similar to that in the original pair of words.

Analysis

It is important that you focus on understanding the *relationship* between the original pair, because this is really what you are trying to parallel.

Notice that you are to select the BEST answer or most similar relationship; therefore, the correct answer may not be directly parallel. The use of the word "best" also implies that there may be more than one good answer.

Categories of Relationship

1. Opposites and Synonyms

    Although a pair of analogies may not be *exact* opposites or *exact* synonyms, a number of pairs may have a roughly opposite or synonymous relationship.

    ERASE : RECORD :: RELINQUISH : ACQUIRE
    PRESENT : INTRODUCE :: SUCCEED : ACCOMPLISH

2. Action/Activity

    Relationship between action and its meaning:
    YAWN : FATIGUE :: SOB : SORROW

    Relationship between action and its performer:
    ORATORY : CANDIDATE :: SOLILOQUY : ACTOR

    Relationship between action and its object:
    HATE : VILLAINY :: WORSHIP : DEITY

    Relationship between action and its recipient:
    DRAMA : AUDIENCE :: WRITING : READER

3. Characteristic/Condition

    Relationship between a characteristic and a related action:
    OPPRESSED : LIBERATION :: MELANCHOLY : CHEER

    Relationship between a characteristic and a related person:
    CRAFTSMANSHIP : ARTISAN :: STATESMANSHIP : GOVERNOR

    Relationship between a characteristic and a related result:
    DISSATISFACTION : COMPLAINT ::
    CURIOSITY : QUESTIONING

4. Effect

Relationship between an effect and its cause:
VERDICT : DELIBERATION :: DEFICIT : OVERSPENDING

Relationship between an effect and its object:
OXIDATION : PAINT :: PHOTOSYNTHESIS : PLANT

5. Time and Space

Relationship between specific and general:
SONNET : LITERATURE :: FOOTBALL : SPORT

Relationship between larger and smaller:
SKYLIGHT : PORTHOLE :: TOME : PAMPHLET

Relationship between younger and older:
SAPLING : TREE :: NEW STAR : NOVA

Relationship between container and contained:
PHOTOGRAPH : IMAGES :: NOVEL : CHAPTERS

Relationship between part and whole:
DIGIT : RATIO :: SYLLABLE : CLAUSE

Relationship between concrete and abstract:
STORY : HEIGHT :: DEGREE : TEMPERATURE

NOTE: Many of these relationships can be presented in a "negative" rather than "positive" sequence. For instance, instead of a pair of words denoting an effect and its cause, you might encounter the *negation* of this relationship, an effect coupled with something that *cannot* be its cause: HAPPINESS : INJURY :: PEACEFULNESS : STRESS. "Happiness is not the effect of injury in the same way as peacefulness is not the effect of stress." The relationship here may be represented as EFFECT : (−) CAUSE, using the minus sign to indicate the negative element in the pair.

Suggested Approach with Samples

1. To determine the relationship between the original pair of words, try to construct a sentence with words that link the pair. *Example:*

RECTANGLE : POLYGON ::
(A) place : occasion
(B) symphony : music
(C) climbing : recreation
(D) triangle : geometry
(E) sight : information

In this case, you might say to yourself, "A rectangle is a kind of polygon," and thus recognize that the relationship here is between specific and general.

2. Narrow your choice to a pair of words that demonstrates *most precisely* the same relationship as the original pair. Test the precision of the relationship by applying the sentence, "A is to B in the same way as C is to D." In the example above, you would say to yourself, "A rectangle is a kind of polygon in the same way as (A) a place is a kind of occasion?—(B) a symphony is a kind of music?—(C) climbing is a kind of recreation?—(D) a triangle is a kind of geometry?—(E) sight is a kind of information?" After following this procedure, the best choices, those that demonstrate the relationship of the original pair, are (B) and (C). To make your final choice, decide which pair of words expresses a "specific to general" relationship that is either *necessary* or *typical.* For instance, climbing is not *necessarily* or *typically* a kind of recreation; however, a symphony is *necessarily* and *typically* a kind of music. Therefore, (B) is the best choice.

3. Often you will need to consider not only the *primary* relationship between the original words, but also a *secondary* relationship as well. *Example:*

TEACHING : LEARNING ::

(A) children : marriage   (D) campaign: victory
(B) food : shopping   (E) test : evaluation
(C) laws : safety

"The object of *teaching* is *learning*." This sentence tells us that the original relationship is between an *action* and its *object:* learning is the object of teaching. Scanning the choices, you see that children *can* be the object of marriage; food *can* be the object of shopping; safety *can* be the object of laws. But in none of these choices—(A), (B), or (C)—is the relationship between the terms *typically* or *necessarily* the relationship of action to object. In choice (D), victory is *necessarily* or *typically* the object of a campaign. In choice (E), evaluation is *necessarily* or *typically* the object of testing. So both of these are possible choices. However, if we consider the secondary relationship or characteristics of the original pair, we notice that learning and teaching typically occur in an *educational* context, and that of the two choices left for consideration, only choice (E) provides a relationship that typically occurs in an educational context. Thus, you should conclude that (E) is the best choice.

To sum up this effective approach to solving analogies:

1. Determine the relationship between the original pair of words by using them in a sentence.

2. Narrow your choices to pairs that typically or necessarily express a similar relationship.
3. Choose the pair that expresses the original relationship most precisely, by taking into account the secondary relationship(s) between the original pair.

SENTENCE COMPLETION

Ability Tested

This section tests your ability to complete sentences with a word or words that retain the meaning of the sentence, and are structurally and stylistically correct.

Basic Skills Necessary

Good reading comprehension skills help in this section, as does a good high school vocabulary.

Directions

Each blank in the following sentences indicates that something has been omitted. Considering the lettered words beneath the sentence, choose the word or set of words that best fits the whole sentence.

Analysis

Note that you must choose the *best* word or words. In cases where several choices *might* fit, prefer the one that fits the meaning of the sentence most precisely. If the sentence contains two blanks, remember that *both* of the words corresponding to your choice must fit.

Suggested Approach With Samples

After reading the sentence and *before* looking at the answer choices, think of words you would insert and look for synonyms to them. *Example:*

Money _____ to a political campaign should be used for political purposes and nothing else.

How would you fill in the blank? Maybe with the word *given* or *donated*? Now look at the choices and find a synonym for *given* or *donated*:

(A) used   (C) contributed   (E) channeled
(B) forwarded   (D) spent

The best choice is (C), *contributed;* it is the nearest synonym to *given* or *donated* and makes good sense in the sentence.

2. Look for signal words. Some signal words are "however," "although," "on the other hand," and "but." *Example:*

Most candidates spend _____ they can raise on their campaigns, but others wind up on election day with a _____ .

(A) so . . . bankroll
(B) time . . . vacation
(C) everything . . . surplus

(D) every cent . . . deficit
(E) nothing . . . war chest

But signals that the first half of the sentence *contrasts* with the second half. The fact that most candidates spend *everything* (and end up with nothing) contrasts with those who end up with a *surplus*. (C) is the correct answer.

3. Watch for contrasts between positive and negative words. Look for words like "not," never," and "no." *Example:*

A virtuous person will not shout _____ in public; he will respect the _____ of other people.

The first blank is obviously a negative word, something a good person would *not* do; the second blank is a positive word, something that a good person *would* do. *Here are the choices:*

(A) obscenities . . . feelings
(B) loudly . . . comfort
(C) anywhere . . . presence

(D) blessings . . . cynicism
(E) insults . . . threat

(B) is neutral-positive; (C) is neutral-neutral; (D) is positive-negative; (E) is negative-negative. Only (A) offers a negative-positive pair of words; (A) is the best choice.

4. Sometimes it is more efficient to work from the second blank first. *Example:*

The merger will eliminate _____ and provide more _____ cross-training of staff.

(A) profit . . . and more
(B) paperwork . . . or less
(C) duplication . . . effective

(D) bosses . . . wasteful
(E) competitors . . . aggressive

The second blank is something that is "provided." Chances are that something provided is a positive word, and *effective* seems like a good choice. Reading choice (C) into the sentence, we find that it makes good sense and is stylistically or structurally correct.

5. What "sounds wrong" should be eliminated. *Example:*

High school students should not be _____ as being immature or naive.

(A) helped   (C) directed   (E) taught
(B) shoved   (D) categorized

The only word that sounds right with "as" is "categorized"; (D) is the best choice.

READING COMPREHENSION

Ability Tested

This section tests your ability to understand, interpret, and analyze reading passages on a variety of topics.

Basic Skills Necessary

Students who have read widely and know how to read and mark a passage actively and efficiently tend to do well on this section.

Directions

Questions follow each of the passages below. Using only the stated or implied information in each passage, answer the questions.

Analysis

1. Answer all the questions for one passage before moving on to the next one. If you don't know the answer, take an educated guess or skip it.
2. Use only the information given or implied in a passage. Do not consider outside information, even if it seems more accurate than the given information.

Suggested Approach With Short Sample Passage

1. Skim the questions first, marking words which give you a clue about what to look for when you read the passage.
2. Skim the passage, reading only the first sentence of each paragraph.
3. Read the passage, marking main points, important conclusions, names, definitions, places, and numbers. Make only a few marks per paragraph.
Passage:

   *By the time a child starts school, he has mastered the major part of the rules of his grammar. He has managed to accomplish this remarkable feat in such a short time by experimenting with and generalizing the rules all by himself. Each child, in effect, rediscovers language in the first few years of his life.

When it comes to vocabulary growth, it is a different story. Unlike grammar, the chief means through which vocabulary is learned is memorization. And some people have a hard time learning and remembering new words.

*—Indicates portions of the passage which refer directly to a question you've skimmed. Also marked are main points and key terms.

1. A child has mastered many rules of grammar by about the age of

(A) 3   (C) 8   (E) 18
(B) 5   (D) 10

The first sentence of the passage contains several words from this question, so it is likely to contain the correct answer. "By the time a child starts school" tells us that the answer is "5." Before choosing (B), you should look at all the answers and cross out those which seem incorrect.

2. Although vocabulary growth involves memorization and grammar-learning doesn't, we may conclude that both vocabulary and grammar make use of:

(A) memorization   (C) words   (E) teachers
(B) study skills   (D) children

The question asks you to simply use your common sense. (A) is incorrect; it contradicts both the passage and the question itself. (D) and (E) make no sense. (B) is a possibility, but (C) is better, because grammar-learning in young children does not necessarily involve study skills, but does involve words.

3. The last sentence in the passage implies that

(A) some people have no trouble learning and remembering new words
(B) some people have a hard time remembering new words
(C) grammar does not involve remembering words
(D) old words are not often remembered
(E) learning and remembering are kinds of growth

"Implies" tells us that the answer is something suggested, but not explicitly stated in the passage. (B) is explicitly stated in the passage, so it may be eliminated. But (B) implies the opposite: if *some* people have a hard time, then it must be true that *some* people don't. (A) is therefore the correct choice. (C), (D), and (E) are altogether apart from the meaning of the last sentence.

COMMON PREFIXES, SUFFIXES, AND ROOTS

The following list should help you to arrive at definitions of unfamiliar words on the Verbal Section of the SAT. These prefixes, suffixes, and roots apply to thousands of words.

Prefixes

Prefix	Meaning	Example
1. pre-	before	precede
2. de-	away, from	deter
3. inter-	between	interstate
4. ob-	against	objection
5. in-	into	instruct
6. mono-	alone, one	monolith
7. epi-	upon	epilogue
8. mis-	wrong	mistake
9. sub-	under	submarine
10. trans-	across, beyond	transcend
11. over-	above	overbearing
12. ad-	to, toward	advance
13. non-	not	nonentity
14. com-	together, with	composite
15. re-	back, again	regress
16. ex-	out of	expel
17. in-	not	insufficient
18. pro-	forward	propel
19. anti-	against	antidote
20. omni-	all, everywhere	omniscient
21. equi-	equal, equally	equivalent
22. homo-	same, equal, like	homogenized
23. semi-	half, partly	semicircle
24. un-	not	unneeded
25. bi-	two	bicycle
26. poly-	many	polymorphous
27. retro-	backward	retrograde
28. mal-	bad	malfunction
29. hyper-	over, too much	hyperactive
30. hypo-	under, too little	hypodermic

Suffixes

Suffix	Meaning	Example
1. -able, -ible	able to	usable
2. -er, -or	one who does	competitor
3. -ism	the practice of	rationalism
4. -ist	one who is occupied with	feminist
5. -less	without, lacking	meaningless
6. -ship	the art or skill of	statesmanship
7. -fy	to make	dignify
8. -ness	the quality of	aggressiveness
9. -tude	the state of	rectitude
10. -logue	a particular kind of speaking or writing	prologue

Roots

Root	Meaning	Example
1. arch	to rule	monarch
2. belli	war, warlike	belligerent
3. bene	good	benevolent
4. chron	time	chronology
5. dic	to say	indicative
6. fac	to make, to do	artifact
7. graph	writing	telegraph
8. mort	to die	mortal
9. port	to carry	deport
10. vid, vis	to see	invisible

Additional Study Aids

For additional review and practice in verbal skills, you will find that *Cliffs Verbal Review for Standardized Tests* will provide you with the help you need. Unlike other general grammar reviews, this book focuses on *standardized test verbal skills* and gives you a practical, personalized test-preparation program. *Cliffs Verbal Review for Standardized Tests* is available at your local bookstore, or you may order it from Cliffs Notes, Inc., by sending in the coupon you'll find at the back of this book.

INTRODUCTION TO MATHEMATICAL ABILITY

The Mathematical Ability sections of the PSAT/NMSQT consist of two basic types of questions; regular Math Ability multiple-choice questions, and Quantitative Comparison (comparisons). The math section is 50 minutes in length and contains 50 problems. Two-thirds to three-quarters of the math problems are of the standard multiple-choice type, with the remaining being comparisons. The Mathematical Ability section generates a scaled score that ranges from 20 to 80, with an average score of about 45 for Juniors later entering college.

A CAREFUL ANALYSIS OF EACH TYPE OF MATHEMATICAL ABILITY QUESTION FOLLOWS.

MATHEMATICAL ABILITY

Ability Tested

The Mathematical Ability section tests your ability to solve mathematical problems involving arithmetic, algebra, and geometry by using problem—solving insight, logic, and application of basic skills.

Basic Skills Necessary

The basic skills necessary to do well on this section include high school algebra and geometry—no formal trigonometry or calculus is necessary. Skills in arithmetic and basic algebra, along with some logical insight into problem-solving situations, are also necessary.

Directions

Solve each problem in this section by using the information given and your own mathematical calculations. Then select the *one* correct answer of the five choices given. Use the available space on the page for scratchwork.

Analysis

All scratchwork is to be done in the test booklet; get used to doing this because no scratch paper is allowed into the testing area.

You are looking for the *one* correct answer; therefore, although other answers may be close, there is never more than one right answer.

Make a special note of the data that may be used for reference *during* this section.

22

Data That May Be Used as Reference for This Section

The area formula for a circle of radius r is: $A = \pi r^2$
The circumference formula is: $C = 2\pi r$
A circle is composed of $360°$.
A straight angle measures $180°$.

Triangle: The sum of the angles of a triangle is $180°$.
If angle ADB is a right angle, then

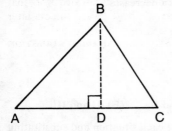

(1) The area of triangle ABC is $\dfrac{AC \times BD}{2}$

(2) $AD^2 + BD^2 = AB^2$

Symbol References:

$=$ is equal to
$\neq$ not equal to
$>$ is greater than
$<$ is less than

$\geq$ is greater than or equal to
$\leq$ is less than or equal to
$\parallel$ is parallel to
$\perp$ is perpendicular to

NOTE: Some problems may be accompanied by figures or diagrams. These figures are drawn as accurately as possible, EXCEPT when it is stated in a specific problem that the figure is not drawn to scale. The figures are meant to provide information useful in solving the problem or problems but are not meant to be measured.

Unless otherwise stated or indicated, all figures lie in a plane.

All numbers used are real numbers.

Suggested Approach With Sample Problems

1. Take advantage of being allowed to mark on the test booklet by always underlining or circling what you are looking for. This will make you sure that you are answering the right question. *Sample:*

If $x + 6 = 9$, then $3x + 1 =$
(A) 3   (B) 9   (C) 10   (D) 34   (E) 46

You should first circle or underline $3x + 1$, because this is what you are solving for. Solving for x leaves $x = 3$ and then substituting into $3x + 1$ gives $3(3) + 1$, or 10. The most common mistake is to solve for x, which is 3, and mistakenly choose (A) as your answer. But remember, you are solving for $3x + 1$, not just x. You should also notice that most of the other choices would all be possible answers if you make common or simple mistakes. The correct answer is (C). *Make   sure that you are answering the right question.*

2. Substituting numbers for variables can often be an aid to understanding a problem. Remember to substitute simple numbers, since *you* have to do the work. *Sample:*

If $x > 1$, which of the following decreases as x decreases?

$$\text{I. } x + x^2$$
$$\text{II. } 2x^2 - x$$
$$\text{III. } \frac{1}{x + 1}$$

(A) I   (B) II   (C) III   (D) I and II   (E) II and III

This problem is most easily solved by taking each situation and substituting simple numbers. However, in the first situation, (I), $x + x^2$, you should recognize that this expression will decrease as x decreases. Trying $x = 2$ gives $2 + (2)^2$, which equals 6. Now trying $x = 3$ gives $3 + (3)^2 = 12$. Notice that choices (B), (C), and (E) are already eliminated because they do not contain I. You should also realize that now you only need to try the values in II; since III is not paired with I as a possible choice, III cannot be one of the answers. Trying $x = 2$ in the expression $2x^2 - x$ gives $2(2)^2 - 2$, or $2(4) - 2$, which leaves 6. Now trying $x = 3$ gives $2(3)^2 - 3$, or $2(9) - 3, = 18 - 3 = 15$. This expression also decreases as x decreases. Therefore the correct answer is (D). Once again notice that III was not even attempted, because it was not one of the possible choices.

3. Sometimes you will immediately recognize the proper formula or method to solve a problem. If this is not the situation, try a reasonable approach and then work from the answers. *Sample:*

Barney can mow the lawn in 5 hours and Fred can mow the lawn in 4 hours. How long will it take them to mow the lawn together?

(A) 5 hours   (C) 4 hours   (E) 1 hour
(B) 4½ hours   (D) 2⅖ hours

Suppose that you are unfamiliar with the type of equation for this problem. Try the "reasonable" method. Since Fred can mow the lawn in 4 hours by himself, he will take less than 4 hours if Barney helps him. Therefore choices (A), (B), and (C) are ridiculous. Taking this method a little further, suppose that Barney could also mow the lawn in 4 hours. Then together it would take Barney and Fred 2 hours. But since Barney is a little slower than this, the total time should be a little more than 2 hours. The correct answer is (D), $2\frac{2}{9}$ hours.

Using the equation for this problem would give the following calculations:

$$\frac{1}{5} + \frac{1}{4} = \frac{1}{x}$$

In 1 hour, Barney could do $\frac{1}{5}$ of the job and in 1 hour Fred could do $\frac{1}{4}$ of the job; unknown (x) is that part of the job they could do together in one hour. Now solving, you calculate as follows:

$$\frac{4}{20} + \frac{5}{20} = \frac{1}{x}$$

$$\frac{9}{20} = \frac{1}{x}$$

Cross multiplying gives 9x = 20
Therefore, x = $\frac{20}{9}$, or $2\frac{2}{9}$.

4. "Pulling" information out of the word problem structure can often give you a better look at what you are working with and therefore you gain additional insight into the problem. *Sample:*

If a mixture is $\frac{3}{7}$ alcohol by volume and $\frac{4}{7}$ water by volume, what is the ratio of the volume of alcohol to the volume of water in this mixture?

(A) $\frac{3}{7}$ (B) $\frac{4}{7}$ (C) $\frac{3}{4}$ (D) $\frac{4}{3}$ (E) $\frac{7}{4}$

The first bit of information that should be pulled out should be what you are looking for: "ratio of the volume of alcohol to the volume of water." Rewrite it as A:W and then into its working form: A/W. Next, you should pull out the volumes of each; A = $\frac{3}{7}$ and W = $\frac{4}{7}$. Now the answer can be easily figured by inspection or substitution: using $(\frac{3}{7})/(\frac{4}{7})$ invert the bottom fraction and multiply to get $\frac{3}{7} \times \frac{7}{4} = \frac{3}{4}$. The ratio of the volume of alcohol to the volume of water is 3 to 4. The correct answer is (C). When pulling out information, actually write out the numbers and/or letters to the side of the problem, putting them into some helpful form and eliminating some of the wording.

5. Sketching diagrams or simple pictures can also be very helpful in

problem solving because the diagram may tip off either a simple solution or a method for solving the problem. *Sample:*

What is the maximum number of pieces of birthday cake of size 4″ by 4″ that can be cut from a cake 20 inches by 20 inches?

(A) 5   (B) 10   (C) 16   (D) 20   (E) 25

Sketching the cake and marking in as follows makes this a fairly simple problem.

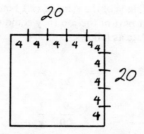

Notice that 5 pieces of cake will fit along each side, therefore 5 × 5 = 25. The correct answer is (E). Finding the total area of the cake and dividing it by the area of one of the 4 x 4 pieces would have also given you the correct answer, but beware of this method because it may not work if the pieces do not fit evenly into the original area.

6. Marking in diagrams as you read them can save you valuable time. Marking can also give you insight into how to solve a problem because you will have the complete picture clearly in front of you. *Sample:*

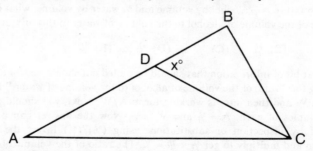

In the triangle, CD is an angle bisector, angle ACD is 30° and angle ABC is a right angle. Find the measurement of angle x in degrees.

(A) 30°   (B) 45°   (C) 60°   (D) 75°   (E) 80°

You should have read the problem and marked as follows:

In the triangle above, CD is an angle bisector (STOP AND MARK IN THE DRAWING), angle ACD is 30° (STOP AND MARK IN THE DRAWING), and angle ABC is a right angle (STOP AND MARK IN THE DRAWING). Find the measurement of angle x in degrees (STOP AND MARK IN OR CIRCLE WHAT YOU ARE LOOKING FOR IN THE DRAWING.).

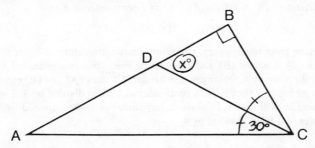

Now with the drawing marked in, it is evident that, since angle ACD is 30°, then angle BCD is also 30° because they are formed by an angle bisector (divides an angle into two equal parts). Since angle ABC is 90° (right angle) and BCD is 30°, then angle x is 60°, because there are 180° in a triangle, $180 - (90 + 30) = 60$. The correct answer is (C). ALWAYS MARK IN DIAGRAMS AS YOU READ THEIR DESCRIPTIONS AND INFORMATION ABOUT THEM. THIS INCLUDES WHAT YOU ARE LOOKING FOR.

7. If it appears that extensive calculations are going to be necessary to solve a problem, check to see how far apart the choices are, and then approximate. The reason for checking the answers first is to give you a guide for how freely you can approximate. *Sample:*

The value for $(.889 \times 55)/9.97$ to the nearest tenth is

(A) .5	(C) 4.9	(E) 49.1
(B) 4.63	(D) 7.7	

Before starting any computations, take a glance at the answers to see how far apart they are. Notice that the only close answers are (B) and (C), except (B) is not a possible choice, since it is to the nearest hundredth, not tenth. Now making some quick approximations $.889 = 1$ and $9.97 = 10$ leaves the problem in this form

$$\frac{1 \times 55}{10} = \frac{55}{10} = 5.5$$

The closest answer is (C), therefore it is the correct answer. Notice that choices (A) and (E) were ridiculous.

8. In some instances, it will be easier to work from the answers. Do not disregard this method because it will at least eliminate some of the choices and could give you the correct answer. *Sample:*

Find the counting number that is less than 15 and when divided by 3 has a remainder of 1 and divided by 4 has a remainder of 2.

(A) 5   (B) 8   (C) 10   (D) 12   (E) 13

By working from the answers, you eliminate wasting time on other numbers from 1 to 14. Choices (B) and (D) can be immediately eliminated because they are divisible by 4, leaving no remainder. Choices (A) and (E) can also be eliminated because they leave a remainder of 1 when divided by 4. Therefore the correct answer is (C); 10 leaves a remainder of 1 when divided by 3 and a remainder of 2 when divided by 4.

QUANTITATIVE COMPARISON

Ability Tested

Quantitative Comparison tests your ability to use mathematical insight, approximation, simple calculation, or common sense to quickly compare two given quantities.

Basic Skills Necessary

This section requires competence in high school arithmetic, algebra, and intuitive geometry. Skills in approximating, comparing, and evaluating are also necessary. No advanced mathematics is necessary.

Directions

In this section you will be given two quantities, one in column A and one in column B. You are to determine a relationship between the two quantities and mark—

(A) if the quantity in column A is greater than the quantity in column B.
(B) if the quantity in column B is greater than the quantity in column A.
(C) if the two quantities are equal.
(D) if the comparison cannot be determined from the information given.

Analysis

The purpose here is to make a comparison; therefore, exact answers are not always necessary. (Remember that you can tell whether you are taller than someone in many cases without knowing that person's height. Comparisons such as this can be made with only partial information—just enough to compare.) (D) is not a possible answer if there are *values* in each column, because you can always compare values.

If you get different relationships, depending on the values you choose for variables, then the answer is always (D). Notice that there are only four possible choices here. *Never* mark (E) on your answer sheet for Quantitative Comparison.

Note that you can add, subtract, multiply, and divide both columns by the same value and the relationship between them will not change. EXCEPTION— You should not multiply or divide each column by negative numbers because then the relationship reverses. Squaring both columns is permissible, as long as each side is positive.

Suggested Approach With Sample Problems

1. This section emphasizes shortcuts, insight, and quick techniques. Long and/or involved mathematical computation is unnecessary and is contrary to the purpose of this section. *Sample:*

Column A	Column B
$21 \times 43 \times 56$	$44 \times 21 \times 57$

Canceling (or dividing) 21 from each side leaves

Column A	Column B
43×56	44×57

The rest of this problem should be done by inspection, because it is obvious that column B is greater than column A without doing any multiplication. You could have attained the correct answer by actually multiplying out each column, but you would then not have enough time to finish the section. The correct answer is (B).

2. The use of partial comparisons can be valuable in giving you insight into finding a comparison. If you cannot simply make a complete comparison, look at each column part by part. *Sample:*

Column A	Column B
$\dfrac{1}{57} - \dfrac{1}{65}$	$\dfrac{1}{58} - \dfrac{1}{63}$

Since finding a common denominator would be too time-consuming, you should first compare the first fraction in each column (partial comparison). Notice that $\frac{1}{57}$ is greater than $\frac{1}{58}$. Now compare the second fractions and notice that $\frac{1}{65}$ is less than $\frac{1}{63}$. Using some common sense and insight, if you start with a larger number and a smaller number, it must be greater than starting with a smaller number and subtracting a larger number, as pointed out below

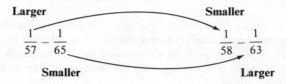

The correct answer is (A).

3. Always keep the column in perspective before starting any calculations. Take a good look at the value in each column before starting to work on one column. *Sample:*

Column A	Column B
$\sqrt[3]{7^6}$	2^8

After looking at each column (Note that the answer could not be (D) because there are values in each column), compute the value on the left. Since you are taking a cube root, simply divide the power of 7 by 3 leaving 7^2, or 49. There is no need to take 2 out to the 8th power, just do as little as necessary: $2^2 = 4, 2^3 = 8, 2^4 = 16, 2^5 = 32$. STOP. It is evident that 2^8 is much greater than 49; the correct answer is (B). Approximating can also be valuable while remembering to keep the columns in perspective.

4. If a problem involves variables (without an equation), substitute in the numbers 0, 1, and -1. Then try $\frac{1}{2}$, and 2 if necessary. Using 0, 1, and -1 will often tip off the answer. *Sample:*

Column A	Column B
$a + b$	ab

Substituting 0 for a and 0 for b gives

$0 + 0$		$0(0)$
Therefore 0	$=$	0

Using these values for a and b gives the answer (C). But anytime you multiply two numbers, it is not the same as when you add them, so try some other values.

Substituting 1 for a and −1 for b gives

$$1 + (-1) \qquad\qquad\qquad\qquad 1(-1)$$

Therefore   0   >   −1

and the answer is now (A).

Anytime you get more than one comparison (different relationships), depending on the values chosen, the correct answer must be (D) (the relationship cannot be determined). Notice that if you had substituted the values a = 4, b = 5; or a = 6, b = 7; or a = 7, b = 9; and so on, you would have repeatedly gotten the answer (B) and might have chosen the incorrect answer.

   5. Oftentimes simplifying one or both columns can make an answer evident. *Sample:*

Column A	Column B
a, b, c, all greater than 0	
a(b + c)	ab + ac

Using the distributive property on column A to simplify, gives ab and ac; therefore, the columns are equal.

   6. Sometimes you can solve for a column directly, in one step, without solving and substituting. If you have to solve an equation or equations to give the columns values, take a second and see if there is a very simple way to get an answer before going through all of the steps. *Sample:*

Column A	Column B
4x + 2 = 10	
2x + 1	4

Hopefully, you would spot that the easiest way to solve for 2x + 1 is directly by dividing 4x + 2 = 10, by 2, leaving 2x + 1 = 5.

Therefore   5   >   4

Solving for x first in the equation, and then substituting, would also have worked, but would have been more time-consuming. The correct answer is (A).

7. Marking diagrams can be very helpful for giving insight into a problem. Remember that figures and diagrams are meant for positional information only. Just because something "looks" larger, is not enough reason to choose an answer. *Sample:*

Column A   **Column B**

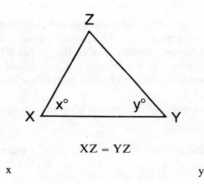

XZ = YZ

x   y

Even though x appears larger, this is not enough. Mark in the diagrams as shown.

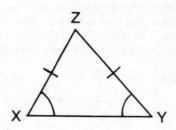

Notice that you should mark things of equal measure with the same markings, and since angles opposite equal sides in a triangle are equal, x = y. The correct answer is (C).

8. If you are given information that is unfamiliar to you and difficult to work with, change the number slightly (but remember what you've changed) to something easier to work with. *Sample:*

Column A	Column B

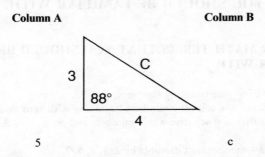

5   c

Since the 88° shown in the figure is unfamiliar to work with, change it to 90° for now, so that you may use the Pythagorean theorem to solve for c.

$$a^2 + b^2 = c^2$$

Solving for c as follows

$$(3)^2 + (4)^2 = c^2$$
$$9 + 16 = c^2$$
$$25 = c^2$$

Therefore
$$5 = c$$

But since you used 90° instead of 88°, you should realize that the side opposite the 88° will be slightly smaller or less than 5. The correct answer is then (A), 5 >c. (Some students may have noticed the 3:4:5 triangle relationship and have not needed the Pythagorean theorem.)

IMPORTANT TERMINOLOGY, FORMULAS, AND GENERAL MATHEMATICAL INFORMATION THAT YOU SHOULD BE FAMILIAR WITH.

COMMON MATH TERMS THAT YOU SHOULD BE FAMILIAR WITH

Natural numbers—the counting numbers: 1, 2, 3, . . .

Whole numbers—the counting numbers beginning with zero: 0, 1, 2, 3, . . .

Integers—positive and negative whole numbers and zero: . . . -3, -2, -1, 0, 1, 2, . . .

Odd numbers—numbers not divisible by 2: 1, 3, 5, 7, . . .

Even numbers—numbers divisible by 2: 0, 2, 4, 6, . . .

Prime number—number divisible by only 1 and itself: 2, 3, 5, 7, 11, 13, . . .

Composite number—number divisible by more than just 1 and itself: 4, 6, 8, 9, 10, 12, 14, 15, . . .

Squares—the result when numbers are multiplied by themselves, ($2 \cdot 2 = 4$) ($3 \cdot 3 = 9$): 1, 4, 9, 16, 25, 36, . . .

Cubes—the result when numbers are multiplied by themselves twice, ($2 \cdot 2 \cdot 2 = 8$), ($3 \cdot 3 \cdot 3 = 27$): 1, 8, 27, . . .

MATH FORMULAS THAT YOU SHOULD BE FAMILIAR WITH

Triangle

Perimeter $= s_1 + s_2 + s_3$

Area $= \frac{1}{2}bh$

Square

Perimeter $= 4s$

Area $= s \cdot s$, or s^2

Rectangle

Perimeter $= 2(b + h)$, or $2b + 2h$

Area $= bh$, or lw

Parallelogram

Perimeter $= 2(l + w)$, or $2l + 2w$

Area $= bh$

Trapezoid

Perimeter $= b_1 + b_2 + s_1 + s_2$

Area $= \frac{1}{2}h(b_1 + b_2)$, or $h\left(\dfrac{b_1 + b_2}{2}\right)$

Circle

Circumference $= 2\pi r$, or πd

Area $= \pi r^2$

Pythagorean theorem (for right triangles) $a^2 + b^2 = c^2$

The sum of the squares of the legs of a right triangle equals the square of the hypotenuse.

Cube	Volume $= s \cdot s \cdot s = s^3$
	Surface area $= s \cdot s \cdot 6$
Rectangular Prism	Volume $= l \cdot w \cdot h$
	Surface area $= 2(lw) + 2(lh) + 2(wh)$

IMPORTANT EQUIVALENTS THAT CAN SAVE YOU TIME

Memorizing the following can eliminate unnecessary computations:

$\frac{1}{100} = .01 = 1\%$

$\frac{1}{10} = .1 = 10\%$

$\frac{1}{5} = \frac{2}{10} = .2 = .20 = 20\%$

$\frac{3}{10} = .3 = .30 = 30\%$

$\frac{2}{5} = \frac{4}{10} = .4 = .40 = 40\%$

$\frac{1}{2} = \frac{5}{10} = .5 = .50 = 50\%$

$\frac{3}{5} = \frac{6}{10} = .6 = .60 = 60\%$

$\frac{7}{10} = .7 = .70 = 70\%$

$\frac{4}{5} = \frac{8}{10} = .8 = .80 = 80\%$

$\frac{9}{10} = .9 = .90 = 90\%$

$\frac{1}{4} = \frac{25}{100} = .25 = 25\%$

$\frac{3}{4} = \frac{75}{100} = .75 = 75\%$

$\frac{1}{3} = .33\frac{1}{3} = 33\frac{1}{3}\%$

$\frac{2}{3} = .66\frac{2}{3} = 66\frac{2}{3}\%$

$\frac{1}{8} = .125 = .12\frac{1}{2} = 12\frac{1}{2}\%$

$\frac{3}{8} = .375 = .37\frac{1}{2} = 37\frac{1}{2}\%$

$\frac{5}{8} = .625 = .62\frac{1}{2} = 62\frac{1}{2}\%$

$\frac{7}{8} = .875 = .87\frac{1}{2} = 87\frac{1}{2}\%$

$\frac{1}{6} = .16\frac{2}{3} = 16\frac{2}{3}\%$

$\frac{5}{6} = .83\frac{1}{3} = 83\frac{1}{3}\%$

$1 = 1.00 = 100\%$

$2 = 2.00 = 200\%$

$3\frac{1}{2} = 3.5 = 3.50 = 350\%$

MEASURES

Customary System, or English System

Length
12 inches (in) = 1 foot (ft)
3 feet = 1 yard (yd)
36 inches = 1 yard
1760 yards = 1 mile (mi)
5280 feet = 1 mile
$5\frac{1}{2}$ yards = 1 rod

Area
144 square inches (sq in) = 1 square foot (sq ft)
9 square feet = 1 square yard (sq yd)

Weight
  16 ounces (oz) = 1 pound (lb)
  2000 pounds = 1 ton (T)

Capacity
  8 fluid ounces (fl oz) = 1 cup (c)
  2 cups = 1 pint (pt)
  2 pints = 1 quart (qt)
  4 quarts = 1 gallon (gal)
  8 dry quarts = 1 peck
  4 pecks = 1 bushel

Time
  365 days = 1 year
  52 weeks = 1 year
  10 years = 1 decade
  100 years = 1 century

Metric System, or The International System of Units
(SI, *Le Système International d'Unités*)

Length—meter
  Kilometer (km) = 1000 meters (m)
  Hectometer (hm) = 100 meters
  Dekameter (dam) = 10 meters

  Meter
  10 decimeters (dm) = 1 meter
  100 centimeters (cm) = 1 meter
  1000 millimeters (mm) = 1 meter

Volume—liter
  Common measures
  1000 milliliters (ml, or mL) = 1 liter (l, or L)
  1000 liters = 1 kiloliter (kl, or kL)

Mass—gram
  Common measures
  1000 milligrams (mg) = 1 gram (g)
  1000 grams = 1 kilogram (kg)
  1000 kilograms = 1 metric ton (t)

WORDS AND PHRASES THAT CAN BE HELPFUL IN SOLVING PROBLEMS

Words that signal an operation:

ADDITION

- Sum
- Total
- Plus
- Increase
- More than
- Greater than

SUBTRACTION

- Difference
- Less
- Decreased
- Reduced
- Fewer
- Have left

MULTIPLICATION

- Of
- Product
- Times
- At (Sometimes)
- Total (Sometimes)

DIVISION

- Quotient
- Divisor
- Dividend
- Ratio
- Parts

GEOMETRY TERMS AND BASIC INFORMATION

Angles

Vertical angles—Formed by two intersecting lines, across from each other, always equal

Adjacent angles—Next to each other, share a common side and vertex

Right angle—Measures 90 degrees

Obtuse angle—Greater than 90 degrees
Acute angle—Less than 90 degrees
Straight angle, or line—Measures 180 degrees
Angle bisector—Divides an angle into two equal angles
Supplementary angles—Two angles whose total is 180 degrees
Complementary angles—Two angles whose total is 90 degrees

Lines

Two points determine a line
Parallel lines—Never meet
Perpendicular lines—Meet at right angles

Polygons

Polygon—A many-sided (more than two) closed plane figure
Regular polygon—A polygon with all sides and all angles equal
Triangle—Three-sided polygon; the interior angles total 180 degrees
    Equilateral triangle—All sides equal
    Isosceles triangle—Two sides equal
    Scalene triangle—All sides of different lengths
    Right triangle—A triangle containing a right angle
In a triangle—Angles opposite equal sides are equal.
In a triangle—The longest side is across from the largest angle, and the shortest side is across from the smallest angle.
In a triangle—The sum of any two sides of a triangle is larger than the third side.
In a triangle—An exterior angle is equal to the sum of the remote two angles.
Median of a triangle—A line segment that connects the vertex and the midpoint of the opposite side.
Quadrilateral—Four-sided polygon; the interior angles total 360 degrees.
    Parallelogram—A quadrilateral with opposite sides parallel
        Rectangle—A parallelogram with all right angles
        Rhombus—A parallelogram with equal sides
        Square—A parallelogram with equal sides and all right angles
    Trapezoid—A quadrilateral with two parallel sides
Pentagon—A five-sided polygon
Hexagon—A six-sided polygon
Octagon—An eight-sided polygon

Circles

Radius of a circle—A line segment from the center of the circle to the circle itself.

Diameter of a circle—A line segment that starts and ends on the circle and goes through the center.

Chord—A line segment that starts and ends on the circle

Arc—A part of the circle

Additional Study Aids

For additional review and practice in math, you will find that *Cliffs Math Review for Standardized Tests* will provide you with the help you need. Unlike other general math reviews, this book focuses on *standardized test math* and gives you a practical, personalized test-preparation program. *Cliffs Math Review for Standardized Tests* is available at your local bookstore, or you may order it from Cliffs Notes, Inc., by sending in the coupon you'll find at the back of this book.

Part III: Practice-Review-Analyze

This section contains one full-length practice simulation PSAT/NMSQT. The practice test is followed by complete answers, explanations, and analysis techniques. The format, levels of difficulty, question structure, and number of questions are similar to those on the actual PSAT. The actual PSAT/NMSQT is copyrighted and may not be duplicated and these questions are not taken directly from the actual test.

When taking this exam, try to simulate the test conditions by following the time allotments carefully. Remember the total test is 1 hour 40 minutes, divided into two sections of 50 minutes each.

FULL-LENGTH PRACTICE TEST

ANSWER SHEET FOR PSAT/NMSQT PRACTICE TEST
(Remove This Sheet and Use It to Mark Your Answers)

START WITH NUMBER 1 FOR EACH NEW SECTION OF THE TEST

SECTION I

CUT HERE

1 Ⓐ Ⓑ Ⓒ Ⓓ Ⓔ	26 Ⓐ Ⓑ Ⓒ Ⓓ Ⓔ	51 Ⓐ Ⓑ Ⓒ Ⓓ Ⓔ
2 Ⓐ Ⓑ Ⓒ Ⓓ Ⓔ	27 Ⓐ Ⓑ Ⓒ Ⓓ Ⓔ	52 Ⓐ Ⓑ Ⓒ Ⓓ Ⓔ
3 Ⓐ Ⓑ Ⓒ Ⓓ Ⓔ	28 Ⓐ Ⓑ Ⓒ Ⓓ Ⓔ	53 Ⓐ Ⓑ Ⓒ Ⓓ Ⓔ
4 Ⓐ Ⓑ Ⓒ Ⓓ Ⓔ	29 Ⓐ Ⓑ Ⓒ Ⓓ Ⓔ	54 Ⓐ Ⓑ Ⓒ Ⓓ Ⓔ
5 Ⓐ Ⓑ Ⓒ Ⓓ Ⓔ	30 Ⓐ Ⓑ Ⓒ Ⓓ Ⓔ	55 Ⓐ Ⓑ Ⓒ Ⓓ Ⓔ
6 Ⓐ Ⓑ Ⓒ Ⓓ Ⓔ	31 Ⓐ Ⓑ Ⓒ Ⓓ Ⓔ	56 Ⓐ Ⓑ Ⓒ Ⓓ Ⓔ
7 Ⓐ Ⓑ Ⓒ Ⓓ Ⓔ	32 Ⓐ Ⓑ Ⓒ Ⓓ Ⓔ	57 Ⓐ Ⓑ Ⓒ Ⓓ Ⓔ
8 Ⓐ Ⓑ Ⓒ Ⓓ Ⓔ	33 Ⓐ Ⓑ Ⓒ Ⓓ Ⓔ	58 Ⓐ Ⓑ Ⓒ Ⓓ Ⓔ
9 Ⓐ Ⓑ Ⓒ Ⓓ Ⓔ	34 Ⓐ Ⓑ Ⓒ Ⓓ Ⓔ	59 Ⓐ Ⓑ Ⓒ Ⓓ Ⓔ
10 Ⓐ Ⓑ Ⓒ Ⓓ Ⓔ	35 Ⓐ Ⓑ Ⓒ Ⓓ Ⓔ	60 Ⓐ Ⓑ Ⓒ Ⓓ Ⓔ
11 Ⓐ Ⓑ Ⓒ Ⓓ Ⓔ	36 Ⓐ Ⓑ Ⓒ Ⓓ Ⓔ	61 Ⓐ Ⓑ Ⓒ Ⓓ Ⓔ
12 Ⓐ Ⓑ Ⓒ Ⓓ Ⓔ	37 Ⓐ Ⓑ Ⓒ Ⓓ Ⓔ	62 Ⓐ Ⓑ Ⓒ Ⓓ Ⓔ
13 Ⓐ Ⓑ Ⓒ Ⓓ Ⓔ	38 Ⓐ Ⓑ Ⓒ Ⓓ Ⓔ	63 Ⓐ Ⓑ Ⓒ Ⓓ Ⓔ
14 Ⓐ Ⓑ Ⓒ Ⓓ Ⓔ	39 Ⓐ Ⓑ Ⓒ Ⓓ Ⓔ	64 Ⓐ Ⓑ Ⓒ Ⓓ Ⓔ
15 Ⓐ Ⓑ Ⓒ Ⓓ Ⓔ	40 Ⓐ Ⓑ Ⓒ Ⓓ Ⓔ	65 Ⓐ Ⓑ Ⓒ Ⓓ Ⓔ
16 Ⓐ Ⓑ Ⓒ Ⓓ Ⓔ	41 Ⓐ Ⓑ Ⓒ Ⓓ Ⓔ	
17 Ⓐ Ⓑ Ⓒ Ⓓ Ⓔ	42 Ⓐ Ⓑ Ⓒ Ⓓ Ⓔ	
18 Ⓐ Ⓑ Ⓒ Ⓓ Ⓔ	43 Ⓐ Ⓑ Ⓒ Ⓓ Ⓔ	
19 Ⓐ Ⓑ Ⓒ Ⓓ Ⓔ	44 Ⓐ Ⓑ Ⓒ Ⓓ Ⓔ	
20 Ⓐ Ⓑ Ⓒ Ⓓ Ⓔ	45 Ⓐ Ⓑ Ⓒ Ⓓ Ⓔ	
21 Ⓐ Ⓑ Ⓒ Ⓓ Ⓔ	46 Ⓐ Ⓑ Ⓒ Ⓓ Ⓔ	
22 Ⓐ Ⓑ Ⓒ Ⓓ Ⓔ	47 Ⓐ Ⓑ Ⓒ Ⓓ Ⓔ	
23 Ⓐ Ⓑ Ⓒ Ⓓ Ⓔ	48 Ⓐ Ⓑ Ⓒ Ⓓ Ⓔ	
24 Ⓐ Ⓑ Ⓒ Ⓓ Ⓔ	49 Ⓐ Ⓑ Ⓒ Ⓓ Ⓔ	
25 Ⓐ Ⓑ Ⓒ Ⓓ Ⓔ	50 Ⓐ Ⓑ Ⓒ Ⓓ Ⓔ	

ANSWER SHEET FOR PSAT/NMSQT PRACTICE TEST
(Remove This Sheet and Use It to Mark Your Answers)

START WITH NUMBER 1 FOR EACH NEW SECTION OF THE TEST

SECTION II

1 Ⓐ Ⓑ Ⓒ Ⓓ Ⓔ	26 Ⓐ Ⓑ Ⓒ Ⓓ Ⓔ	51 Ⓐ Ⓑ Ⓒ Ⓓ Ⓔ
2 Ⓐ Ⓑ Ⓒ Ⓓ Ⓔ	27 Ⓐ Ⓑ Ⓒ Ⓓ Ⓔ	52 Ⓐ Ⓑ Ⓒ Ⓓ Ⓔ
3 Ⓐ Ⓑ Ⓒ Ⓓ Ⓔ	28 Ⓐ Ⓑ Ⓒ Ⓓ Ⓔ	53 Ⓐ Ⓑ Ⓒ Ⓓ Ⓔ
4 Ⓐ Ⓑ Ⓒ Ⓓ Ⓔ	29 Ⓐ Ⓑ Ⓒ Ⓓ Ⓔ	54 Ⓐ Ⓑ Ⓒ Ⓓ Ⓔ
5 Ⓐ Ⓑ Ⓒ Ⓓ Ⓔ	30 Ⓐ Ⓑ Ⓒ Ⓓ Ⓔ	55 Ⓐ Ⓑ Ⓒ Ⓓ Ⓔ
6 Ⓐ Ⓑ Ⓒ Ⓓ Ⓔ	31 Ⓐ Ⓑ Ⓒ Ⓓ Ⓔ	56 Ⓐ Ⓑ Ⓒ Ⓓ Ⓔ
7 Ⓐ Ⓑ Ⓒ Ⓓ Ⓔ	32 Ⓐ Ⓑ Ⓒ Ⓓ Ⓔ	57 Ⓐ Ⓑ Ⓒ Ⓓ Ⓔ
8 Ⓐ Ⓑ Ⓒ Ⓓ Ⓔ	33 Ⓐ Ⓑ Ⓒ Ⓓ Ⓔ	58 Ⓐ Ⓑ Ⓒ Ⓓ Ⓔ
9 Ⓐ Ⓑ Ⓒ Ⓓ Ⓔ	34 Ⓐ Ⓑ Ⓒ Ⓓ Ⓔ	59 Ⓐ Ⓑ Ⓒ Ⓓ Ⓔ
10 Ⓐ Ⓑ Ⓒ Ⓓ Ⓔ	35 Ⓐ Ⓑ Ⓒ Ⓓ Ⓔ	60 Ⓐ Ⓑ Ⓒ Ⓓ Ⓔ
11 Ⓐ Ⓑ Ⓒ Ⓓ Ⓔ	36 Ⓐ Ⓑ Ⓒ Ⓓ Ⓔ	61 Ⓐ Ⓑ Ⓒ Ⓓ Ⓔ
12 Ⓐ Ⓑ Ⓒ Ⓓ Ⓔ	37 Ⓐ Ⓑ Ⓒ Ⓓ Ⓔ	62 Ⓐ Ⓑ Ⓒ Ⓓ Ⓔ
13 Ⓐ Ⓑ Ⓒ Ⓓ Ⓔ	38 Ⓐ Ⓑ Ⓒ Ⓓ Ⓔ	63 Ⓐ Ⓑ Ⓒ Ⓓ Ⓔ
14 Ⓐ Ⓑ Ⓒ Ⓓ Ⓔ	39 Ⓐ Ⓑ Ⓒ Ⓓ Ⓔ	64 Ⓐ Ⓑ Ⓒ Ⓓ Ⓔ
15 Ⓐ Ⓑ Ⓒ Ⓓ Ⓔ	40 Ⓐ Ⓑ Ⓒ Ⓓ Ⓔ	65 Ⓐ Ⓑ Ⓒ Ⓓ Ⓔ
16 Ⓐ Ⓑ Ⓒ Ⓓ Ⓔ	41 Ⓐ Ⓑ Ⓒ Ⓓ Ⓔ	
17 Ⓐ Ⓑ Ⓒ Ⓓ Ⓔ	42 Ⓐ Ⓑ Ⓒ Ⓓ Ⓔ	
18 Ⓐ Ⓑ Ⓒ Ⓓ Ⓔ	43 Ⓐ Ⓑ Ⓒ Ⓓ Ⓔ	
19 Ⓐ Ⓑ Ⓒ Ⓓ Ⓔ	44 Ⓐ Ⓑ Ⓒ Ⓓ Ⓔ	
20 Ⓐ Ⓑ Ⓒ Ⓓ Ⓔ	45 Ⓐ Ⓑ Ⓒ Ⓓ Ⓔ	
21 Ⓐ Ⓑ Ⓒ Ⓓ Ⓔ	46 Ⓐ Ⓑ Ⓒ Ⓓ Ⓔ	
22 Ⓐ Ⓑ Ⓒ Ⓓ Ⓔ	47 Ⓐ Ⓑ Ⓒ Ⓓ Ⓔ	
23 Ⓐ Ⓑ Ⓒ Ⓓ Ⓔ	48 Ⓐ Ⓑ Ⓒ Ⓓ Ⓔ	
24 Ⓐ Ⓑ Ⓒ Ⓓ Ⓔ	49 Ⓐ Ⓑ Ⓒ Ⓓ Ⓔ	
25 Ⓐ Ⓑ Ⓒ Ⓓ Ⓔ	50 Ⓐ Ⓑ Ⓒ Ⓓ Ⓔ	

CUT HERE

SECTION I: VERBAL ABILITY

Time: 50 Minutes
65 Questions

In this section, choose the best answer for each question and blacken the corresponding space on the answer sheet.

Antonyms

DIRECTIONS

Each word in CAPITAL LETTERS is followed by five words or phrases. The correct choice is the word or phrase whose meaning is most nearly *opposite* to the meaning of the word in capitals. You may be required to distinguish fine shades of meaning. Look at all choices before marking your answer.

1. HUMANE
   (A) indecent
   (B) barbarous
   (C) delinquent
   (D) criminal
   (E) terrible

2. BELLICOSE
   (A) varicose
   (B) ugly
   (C) ringing
   (D) peaceful
   (E) calm

3. INEFFABLE
   (A) dictatable
   (B) separable
   (C) cogent
   (D) definable
   (E) ethereal

4. REPULSIVE
   (A) putrid
   (B) attentive
   (C) attractive
   (D) constructive
   (E) divergent

5. FABLE
   (A) fact
   (B) story
   (C) dream
   (D) anthology
   (E) journal

47

6. DEPORT
   (A) port
   (B) depart
   (C) welcome
   (D) import
   (E) portable

7. MATRIARCH
   (A) archduke
   (B) hierarchy
   (C) patrimonial
   (D) patriarch
   (E) oligarchy

8. CREDULOUS
   (A) incredible
   (B) inconceivable
   (C) unconvinceable
   (D) unremarkable
   (E) small

9. POETICAL
   (A) mysterious
   (B) outstanding
   (C) literary
   (D) novelistic
   (E) prosaic

10. PROSELYTE
    (A) vandal
    (B) electrolyte
    (C) disciple
    (D) apostate
    (E) renegade

Analogies

DIRECTIONS

In each question below, you are given a related pair of words or phrases. Select the lettered pair that *best* expresses a relationship similar to that in the original pair of words.

11. MOUNTAIN : PEAK : :
    (A) peak : Himalayas
    (B) hill : ridge
    (C) building : roof
    (D) valley : pass
    (E) sky : cloud

12. GEOMETRY : TRIANGLE : :
    (A) circle : shape
    (B) botany : daisy
    (C) teacher : education
    (D) algebra : trigonometry
    (E) history : future

13. OBVIOUS : EVIDENT : :
    - (A) obliterated : obligated
    - (B) fraudulent : funny
    - (C) hobbled : awkward
    - (D) covert : open
    - (E) allowed : granted

14. DRY : PARCHED : :
    - (A) dishonest : crooked
    - (B) wet : soaked
    - (C) swampy : sere
    - (D) horrendous : ugly
    - (E) livid : angry

15. DIGIT : HAND : :
    - (A) pancreas : skeleton
    - (B) plateau : mountains
    - (C) key : typewriter
    - (D) railroad : junction
    - (E) sun : star

16. POOR MAN : SLUM : :
    - (A) ship : water
    - (B) air force : airplane
    - (C) placebo : medicine
    - (D) pirouette : whirl
    - (E) planetarium : spaceship

17. CAR : IGNITION : :
    - (A) airplane : wing
    - (B) dirigible : propeller
    - (C) kibosh : weapon
    - (D) larynx : epiglottis
    - (E) light : switch

18. BESTIAL : BRUTISH : :
    - (A) monstrous : simian
    - (B) frivolous : trivial
    - (C) heavy : heavier
    - (D) smiling : smirking
    - (E) medial : extreme

19. EDIFYING : ENLIGHTENING : :
    - (A) eating : spitting
    - (B) entertaining : electrifying
    - (C) instructing : teaching
    - (D) publishing : writing
    - (E) exercising : optioning

20. MONOTHEISM : THEISM : :
    - (A) monologue : prologue
    - (B) unicycle : cycle
    - (C) banality : vanity
    - (D) unity : unification
    - (E) monocle : glasses

Sentence Completion

DIRECTIONS

Each blank in the following sentences indicates that something has been omitted. Consider the lettered words beneath the sentence and choose the word or set of words that best fits the whole sentence.

21. Rural dwellers who hold _____ values may, at times, be altogether uncritical of the various federal programs aimed at the regulation and _____ of agriculture.
    (A) rigorous . . . legalization
    (B) conventional . . . subsidization
    (C) ludicrous . . . obfuscation
    (D) rhythmic . . . communization
    (E) similarity . . . decimation

22. The starfish is a radially _____ animal with arms or rays arising from a central portion called the disc.
    (A) rubberized   (D) rectangular
    (B) obtuse   (E) symmetrical
    (C) stenographic

23. The population of a species at any given time is determined by the ratio of the biotic _____ to environmental resistance.
    (A) jeopardy   (D) lexicon
    (B) potential   (E) annoyance
    (C) excitement

24. *Rite of Passage* is a good novel by any standards; _____, it should rank high on any list of science fiction.
    (A) consistently   (D) consequently
    (B) invariably   (E) fortunately
    (C) lingeringly

25. When one is thrust into an unknown world, he is careful to note the conditions in which he finds himself, _____ them with his _____.
    (A) bemusing . . . daydreams   (D) concurring . . . thoughts
    (B) refuting . . . expertise   (E) comparing . . . expectations
    (C) congealing . . . observations

26. He does not accept what he is told readily—he is suspicious, he is cautious, he is _____, and he is analytical.
    (A) confounded   (D) qualified
    (B) colossal   (E) skeptical
    (C) crass

27. Mr. Hoffer's primary criticism of Jack is that he is _____ and lacks the personal drive to make something of the many opportunities afforded him.
(A) pugnacious   (D) indecisive
(B) odious   (E) peculiarity
(C) transgression

28. The decorum of the legislative meeting was quickly _____ by his _____ tactics.
(A) enhanced . . . devious
(B) truncated . . . truant
(C) vexed . . . vicious
(D) exaggerated . . . boisterous
(E) vitiated . . . dilatory

29. Due to their bitter rivalry, Peter found it necessary to _____ the process by which Floyd reached his conclusions concerning human behavior under stress.
(A) dilate   (D) thwart
(B) deprecate   (E) discuss
(C) enunciate

30. In his large, _____ home, he was able to _____ himself from the rigors of urban life.
(A) palatial . . . sequester   (D) inconsiderable . . . hide
(B) rambunctious . . . isolate   (E) dashing . . . stigmatize
(C) colonial . . . dignify

Reading Comprehension

DIRECTIONS

Questions follow each of the passages below. Using only the stated or implied information in each passage, answer the questions.

The Nellie, a cruising yawl, swung to her anchor without a flutter of the sails, and was at rest. The flood had made, the wind was nearly calm, and being bound down the river, the only thing for it was to come to and wait for the turn of the tide.

The sea-reach of the Thames stretched before us like the beginning of an interminable waterway. In the offing the sea and the sky were welded together without a joint, and in the luminous space the tanned sails of the barges drifting up with the tide seemed to stand still in red clusters of canvas sharply peaked, with gleams of varnished sprits. A haze rested on the low shores that ran out to sea in vanishing flatness.

The air was dark above Gravesend, and farther back still seemed condensed into a mournful gloom, brooding motionless over the biggest, and the greatest, town on earth.

The Director of Companies was our captain and our host. We four affectionately watched his back as he stood in the bows looking to seaward. On the whole river there was nothing that looked half so nautical. He resembled a pilot, which to a seaman is trustworthiness personified. It was difficult to realize his work was not out there in the luminous estuary, but behind him, within the brooding gloom.

Between us there was, as I have already said somewhere, the bond of the sea. Besides holding our hearts together through long periods of separation, it had the effect of making us tolerant of each other's yarns—and even convictions. The Lawyer—the best of old fellows— had, because of his many years and many virtues, the only cushion on deck, and was lying on the only rug. The Accountant had brought out already a box of dominoes, and was toying architecturally with the bones. Marlow sat cross-legged right aft, leaning against the mizzen-mast. He had sunken cheeks, a yellow complexion, a straight back, an ascetic aspect, and, with his arms dropped, the palms of hands outwards, resembled an idol. The Director, satisfied the anchor had good hold, made his way aft and sat down amongst us. We exchanged a few words lazily. Afterwards there was silence on board the yacht. For some reason or other we did not begin that game of dominoes. We felt meditative, and fit for nothing but placid staring. The day was ending in a serenity of still and exquisite brilliance. The water shone pacifically; the sky, without a speck, was a benign immensity of unstained light; the very mist on the Essex marsh was like a gauzy and radiant fabric, hung from the wooded rises inland, and draping the low shores in diaphanous folds. Only the gloom to the west, brooding over the upper reaches, became more sombre every minute, as if angered by the approach of the sun.

And at last, in its curved and imperceptible fall, the sun sank low, and from glowing white changed to a dull red without rays and without heat, as if about to go out suddenly, stricken to death by the touch of that gloom brooding over a crowd of men.

31. The last paragraph describes
    (A) man's destruction of the sun
    (B) a sunrise
    (C) a change of seasons
    (D) a sunset
    (E) the death of a crowd of men

32. How many men are aboard the *Nellie*?
    (A) four   (D) cannot be determined
    (B) five   (E) more than five
    (C) three

33. In paragraph 4, "bones" is another word for
    (A) the architecture of the accountant's hands
    (B) the skeletons which emerge at sunset
    (C) Marlow
    (D) the plants which make up the deck
    (E) dominoes

34. The author implies that each of the passengers is a former
    (A) seaman
    (B) storyteller
    (C) idol
    (D) pilot
    (E) personification of trustworthiness

35. The *Nellie* is
    (A) not moving
    (B) fluttering
    (C) stretching down the interminable waterway
    (D) becoming increasingly gloomy
    (E) a government vessel

    The units that control heredity are called genes. A gene is not directly observable. But we can observe within the nucleus of a cell the filament-like bodies which carry the genetic material. These bodies are called chromosomes ("color bodies"). Chromosomes ordinarily exist in pairs (except for the sex chromosomes). During regular cell division (mitosis) a chromosome divides in two. A pair then goes to each of the daughter cells which have resulted from cell division. During reduction division (meiosis), the chromosome pairs—instead of dividing themselves again—merely line up and then move away from each other, so that each mature sex cell carries only half the normal number of chromosomes (haploid number). The haploid number of chromosomes in man is 23. When a mature male sex cell unites with a mature female sex cell during fertilization, each contributes its share of chromosomes, thus restoring to the fertilized ovum (zygote) the normal (or diploid) number of chromosomes. The diploid number of chromosomes in man is 46. Changes in the structure of a gene (with a resultant difference in the expression of the gene in the phenotype) are called mutations. Mutations occur accidentally. But once they have occurred, they will be inherited indefinitely until another mutation occurs.

The sum total of genes within an organism is called the genotype. We cannot experiment with or observe a genotype. We can only deal with the observable characters of an organism. The sum total of the observable characters of an organism is called the phenotype. A phenotype is the result of the interaction between environmental forces and the genotype. The phenotype is the most important factor in evolution, for it is acted upon by natural selection and it is directly responsible for specialization.

Adaptation is the ability of an organism to live in a given environment. This ability is flexible. But there are absolute limits which must be met if an organism is to survive at all.

Traits vary from one population to another. It is believed that most of these traits have arisen as a response to the environment. Thus they are of adaptive value. We must bear in mind that these traits, once established in a population, are inherited. Therefore, a race may be defined as a population within a species that varies from other such breeding populations in the frequency of its genes. It is not surprising to note that the geographical populations of mankind are physically distinct. The frequency of traits seen in mankind throughout the world form a continuum, variations between contiguous populations being very gradual and barely perceptible. We call the zones of similar frequencies within the continuum clines. Traits seem to distribute throughout the world relatively independent of one another.

36. The information given in the first paragraph is probably not a result of
    (A) an authoritative study of cell reproduction
    (B) putting together some basic scientific knowledge
    (C) carefully watching chromosomes during meiosis and mitosis, under an electron microscope
    (D) carefully watching genes during meiosis and mitosis, under an electron microscope
    (E) someone's curiosity about cell reproduction

37. A region characterized by extreme cold might affect its inhabitants'
    (A) genotype   (D) mutations
    (B) phenotype   (E) mitosis
    (C) haploid number

38. Phenotype has something important in common with
    (A) absolute limits   (D) traits
    (B) continuum   (E) mankind
    (C) geographical populations

39. The general subject of this passage might be
   (A) electrical engineering   (D) philosophy
   (B) nuclear power   (E) anthropology
   (C) physics

   Economic growth involves both benefits and costs. The desirability of increasing production has frequently been challenged in recent years, and some have even maintained that economic growth is merely a quantitative enlargement that has no human meaning or value. However, economic growth is an increase in the capacity to produce goods and services that people want. Since the product of economic growth can be measured by its value to someone, it is important to ask whose standard of valuation counts.

   In the United States, the value of a product is what purchasers pay for it. This is determined by the purchasers' preferences combined with conditions of supply, which in turn reflect various other factors, such as natural and technological circumstances at any given time and the preferences of those who supply capital and labor. The value by which we measure a product synthesizes all these factors. Gross National Product (GNP) is the market value of the nation's total output of goods and services.

   Gross National Product is not a perfect measure of all the activities involved in economic output. It does not account for deteriorations or improvements in the environment, even when they are incidental results of the production process. On the other hand, it does not count as "product" many benefits provided as side effects of the economic process; it does not include productive but unpaid work (such as that done by a housewife); and it does not reckon with such other factors as the burdensomeness of work, the length of the work week, and so forth.

   Nonetheless, the GNP concept makes an important contribution to our understanding of how the economy is working. While it is not a complete measure of economic productivity and even less so of "welfare," the level and rate of increase of the GNP are clearly and positively associated with what most people throughout the world see as an improvement in the quality of life.

   Although there has been much soul-searching about the role of increasing material affluence in the good life, it seems quite certain that most Americans prefer a rapidly growing GNP and its consequences. This does not mean that growth of the GNP is an absolute that must be furthered at all costs. Growth of the GNP has its costs, and beyond a certain point they are not worth paying. Moreover, people want things that are not measured in the GNP. Still, while human values and conditions of life change, and might conceivably make the social cost of a rising GNP seem too high, it is likely that we would still be concerned about the growth of our nation's GNP.

In any case, since there is little evidence of a decline in the value assigned to economic output as a whole, the factors that influence our capacity to produce remain of great importance. In the long run, the same factors result in a growing GNP and in other social benefits: size and competence of population, state of knowledge, amount of capital, and the effectiveness with which these are combined and utilized.

The average rate of economic growth in the United States has been exceptionally high. In the mid-nineteenth century, per capita real incomes in this country and in the industralized countries of Europe were roughly equal. In mid-twentieth century, however, real per capita income in the United States was double that in the advanced countries of Europe, and in the 1970s the growth of real per capita income in the United States is expected to surpass the historical average. This will result mainly from an unusually rapid growth in the size of the labor force relative to the population as a whole. It is uncertain, however, whether this will lead to increases in the rate of individual productivity.

A country's annual outflow of goods and services depends on these three factors:

1. The quantity and quality of the factors of production.
2. The efficiency with which these factors are used.
3. The extent of utilization of the potential capacity of the economy.

Within this framework it is possible to point out both the shortcomings and the advantages of developed and developing nations in the growth race.

40. The United States GNP is more than double that of the advanced European countries; this does not necessarily mean that
    (A) the average rate of economic growth in the U.S. has been high
    (B) the U.S. output of goods and services exceeds that of European countries
    (C) the U.S. enjoys greater material affluence than the European countries
    (D) European households are maintained less efficiently than American households
    (E) European countries have a lower GNP than does the U.S.

41. Someone opposed to furthering growth of the GNP might instead favor
    (A) a longer work week   (D) development of native lands
    (B) both benefits and costs   (E) an emphasis on the spiritual
    (C) material growth   growth of American citizens

42. We might assume that the author favors continuing growth of the GNP because
    (A) although he mentions that the GNP has its costs, he does not list those costs
    (B) he is not a housewife
    (C) he is unlike most people throughout the world
    (D) he does not believe in perfect measures of economic growth
    (E) he prefers things as they were in 19th century

43. Those who decide the value of a product are
    (A) the GNP   (D) its inventors
    (B) economic theorists   (E) its purchasers
    (C) its naysayers

44. The factor which does not influence the growth of the GNP is
    (A) the condition of the population
    (B) the American dependence upon soul-searching
    (C) the capital available in the country
    (D) knowledge related to production of goods and services
    (E) the efficiency of the production process

Today the study of language in our schools is somewhat confused. It is the most traditional of scholastic subjects being taught in a time when many of our traditions no longer fit our needs. You to whom these pages are addressed speak English and are therefore in a worse case than any other literate people.

People pondering the origin of language for the first time usually arrive at the conclusion that it developed gradually as a system of conventionalized grunts, hisses, and cries and must have been a very simple affair in the beginning. But when we observe the language behavior of what we regard as primitive cultures, we find it strikingly elaborate and complicated. Stefansson, the explorer, said that "In order to get along reasonably well an Eskimo must have at the tip of his tongue a vocabulary of more than 10,000 words, much larger than the active vocabulary of an average businessman who speaks English. Moreover these Eskimo words are far more highly inflected than those of any of the well-known European languages, for a single noun can be spoken or written in several hundred different forms, each having a precise meaning different from that of any other. The forms of the verbs are even more numerous. The Eskimo language is, therefore, one of the most difficult in the world to learn, with the result that almost no traders or explorers have even tried to learn it. Consequently there has grown up, in intercourse between Eskimos and whites, a jargon similar to the pidgin English used in China, with a vocabulary of from 300 to 600 uninflected words, most of them derived from Eskimo but some derived from English, Danish, Spanish, Hawaiian and other languages. It is this jargon which is usually referred to by travellers as 'the Eskimo language.'"[1] And Professor Thalbitzer of Copenhagen, who did take the trouble to learn Eskimo, seems to endorse the explorer's view when he writes: "The language is polysynthetic. The grammar is extremely rich in flexional forms, the conjugation of a common verb being served by about 350 suffixes, equivalent to personal pronouns and verb endings. For the declension of a noun there are 150 suffixes (for dual and plural, local cases, and possessive flexion). The demonstrative pronouns have a separate flexion. The derivative endings effective in the vocabulary and the construction of sentences or sentence-like words amount to at least 250. Notwithstanding all these constructive peculiarities, the grammatical and synthetic system is remarkably concise and, in its own way, logical."[2]

[1] *The Encyclopaedia Britannica,* Fourteenth Edition, Vol. 8, p. 709.
[2] Ibid., p. 707.

45. The size of the Eskimo language spoken by most whites is
    (A) spoken in England, Denmark, Spain, and Hawaii
    (B) less than the size of the language spoken by Eskimos
    (C) highly inflected
    (D) inestimable
    (E) irrelevant

46. Some of the evidence about language in the passage is taken from the observations of
    (A) linguists   (D) an explorer
    (B) Eskimos   (E) primitive cultures
    (C) businessmen

47. The passage implies that a "traditional" course in today's schools would be
    (A) Advances in Biology: The Creation of Artificial Life
    (B) Social Revolution in America
    (C) The History of the English Language
    (D) Television and Its Impact
    (E) Disco Dancing as Psychotherapy

48. According to the passage, the language of primitive cultures was
    (A) nonexistent
    (B) only spoken by Eskimos
    (C) monosyllabic
    (D) simpleminded
    (E) elaborate and complicated

49. The author's overall point is that primitive languages
    (A) may be large, complex, and complicated
    (B) may be large, complex, and logical
    (C) may be large, old, and logical
    (D) may be similar to pidgin English
    (E) tell us little about the origin of language

50. In this passage, the word "inflection" means
    (A) the suffixes added on to a verb or noun
    (B) a sophisticated pidgin English
    (C) a conventionalized system of grunts and hisses
    (D) inflicted
    (E) changes in the form and meaning of a word

Antonyms

Select the word or phrase whose meaning is most nearly *opposite* to the meaning of the word in capitals.

51. SUPPLICATION
    (A) flexibility   (C) grant   (E) implication
    (B) plethora   (D) surplus

52. REDEEM
    (A) release   (C) imprison   (E) harm
    (B) condemn   (D) satanize

53. PRUDENCE
    (A) folly   (C) providence (E) liberty
    (B) circumspection   (D) forecast

54. DISTEND
    (A) enjoin   (C) inherit   (E) contend
    (B) deflate   (D) conflate

55. LUXURIANT
    (A) green   (C) small   (E) uncivilized
    (B) sedate   (D) miserly

Analogies

Select the lettered pair which best expresses a relationship similar to that expressed in the original pair.

56. OPAQUE : CLEAR : :
    (A) authentic : false
    (B) clement : mean
    (C) quiet : tranquil
    (D) knowledgeable : erudite
    (E) genuine : true

57. TIGER : CARNIVORE : :
    (A) stove : kitchen
    (B) train : vehicle
    (C) vastness : quantity
    (D) parakeet : parrot
    (E) offense : unpleasantry

58. JAUNTY : PERKY : :
    (A) agile : political
    (B) caustic : witty
    (C) lackluster : vital
    (D) diagonal : horizontal
    (E) par : equal

59. AMBIGUOUS : CLEAR : :
    (A) unabridged : free
    (B) singular : unusual
    (C) synthetic : diametric
    (D) ambivalent : dextrous
    (E) indefinite : definite

60. ANARCHY : UNCONTROLLED : :
    (A) mob : orderly
    (B) gathering : nonviolent
    (C) student : misguided
    (D) oligarchy : controlled
    (E) hierarchy : patriarchal

Sentence Completion

Select the word or word set which *best* completes each of the following sentences.

61. The _____ among the workers lowered productivity in a _____ way.
    (A) implication . . . rebellious
    (B) impiety . . . dangerous
    (C) malaise . . . harrowing
    (D) tedious . . . terrible
    (E) vigor . . . stimulating

62. I cannot _____ why Steve insists he is a novice at tennis.
    (A) insinuate
    (B) find
    (C) fulminate
    (D) fathom
    (E) convince

63. One cannot _____ to be impressed by the structural
    and _____ differences between the United States as a federal
    union in 1789 and the United States as a federal union today.
    (A) deteriorate . . . legal
    (B) stop . . . attitudinal
    (C) begin . . . politically
    (D) fail . . . operational
    (E) start . . . classical

64. I cannot begin to _____ a story as wild and
    _____ as the one Jack told us Thursday evening.
    (A) create . . . foolhardy
    (B) fabricate . . . unbelievable
    (C) invent . . . sanguine
    (D) communicate . . . falsehood
    (E) legislate . . . crazy

65. Our senses reveal the way things appear when _____ through
    the sense _____ and the intellect reveals the way they appear
    to the mind that thinks about them; but neither the senses nor the
    intellect tells us anything about the nature of objects as they exist apart
    from our knowing about them.
    (A) known . . . reflections
    (B) seen . . . liabilities
    (C) felt . . . functions
    (D) predicated . . . activity
    (E) experienced . . . organs

SECTION II: MATHEMATICAL ABILITY

Time: 50 Minutes
50 Questions

DIRECTIONS

Solve each problem in this section by using the information given and your own mathematical calculations. Then select the *one* correct answer of the five choices given. Use the available space on the page for scratchwork.

Data That May Be Used as Reference for This Section

The area formula for a circle of radius r is: $A = \pi r^2$
The circumference formula is: $C = 2\pi r$
A circle is composed of 360°.
A straight angle measures 180°.

Triangle: The sum of the angles of a triangle is 180°.
If angle ADB is a right angle, then

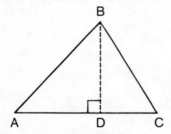

(1) The area of triangle ABC is $\dfrac{AC \times BD}{2}$

(2) $AD^2 + BD^2 = AB^2$

Symbol References:
= is equal to
≠ not equal to
> is greater than
< is less than

≥ is greater than or equal to
≤ is less than or equal to
‖ is parallel to
⊥ is perpendicular to

NOTE: Some problems may be accompanied by figures or diagrams. These figures are drawn as accurately as possible, EXCEPT when it is stated in a specific problem that the figure is not drawn to scale. The figures are meant to provide information useful in solving the problem or problems but are not meant to be measured.

Unless otherwise stated or indicated, all figures lie in a plane.

All numbers used are real numbers.

1. If $3x + 6y = 21$, then $x + 2y =$
   (A) $7 - 2y$ (B) $7/2$ (C) 7 (D) $21 - 6y$
   (E) Cannot be determined.

2. Find the sum of $1\frac{1}{5}$ and its reciprocal.
   (A) 0 (B) $1\frac{2}{3}$ (C) $2\frac{1}{30}$ (D) $2\frac{2}{5}$ (E) $7\frac{1}{5}$

3. What is the area in square feet of a circle inscribed in a square having a side of 10 feet?
   (A) 10π (B) 20π (C) 25π (D) 100π (E) 200π

4. On a clock, if the minute hand starts at the 12, goes around twice, and stops at the 3, then it has traversed how many total degrees?
   (A) $90°$ (B) $450°$ (C) $720°$ (D) $800°$ (E) $810°$

5. If $m + 5$ is an even integer, which of the following is not an even integer?
   (A) $m - 1$ (B) m (C) $m + 1$ (D) $2m + 10$
   (E) $3m + 1$

6. If Tom leaves home and travels west for 3 miles and then north for 4 miles, how far is he from home?
   (A) 1 mile   (B) $3\frac{1}{2}$ miles   (C) 4 miles   (D) 5 miles
   (E) 7 miles

7. $\dfrac{1/2 + 1/3 + 1/4}{1/4 + 1/6 + 1/12} =$

   (A) $2\frac{4}{9}$ (B) $2\frac{1}{6}$ (C) $\frac{6}{13}$ (D) $\frac{9}{22}$ (E) $\frac{1}{12}$

8. Which of the following is NEVER true?
   I. The sum of 2 even integers is even.
   II. The product of 2 even integers is even.
   III. The sum of 2 odd integers is odd.
   IV. The sum of 3 odd integers is even.

   (A) I and II   (B) II and III   (C) III and IV
   (D) I and III   (E) II and IV

9. If it takes a machine ⅔ of a minute to produce one item, how many items will it produce in 2 hours?

   (A) ⅓   (B) ⁴⁄₃   (C) 80   (D) 120   (E) 180

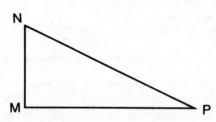

10. On △MNP, MN ⊥ MP, MP = 24, and NP = 26. Find the area of MNP in square units.

    (A) 60   (B) 120   (C) 240   (D) 312
    (E) cannot be determined

11. When a certain integer J is divided by 5, the remainder is 1. When integer J is divided by 3, then the remainder is 2. The value for J is

    (A) 6   (B) 11   (C) 12   (D) 16   (E) 21

12. $\dfrac{(2/3)^2 - 3}{2 - (.5)^2} =$

    (A) $\dfrac{102}{63}$ (B) $\dfrac{92}{63}$ (C) $\dfrac{63}{92}$ (D) $-\dfrac{92}{63}$ (D) $-\dfrac{102}{63}$

13. If two numbers have only the number 1 as a common divisor, then they are called "relatively prime." Which of the following are NOT relatively prime?

    I. 3   II. 4   III. 7   IV. 12

    (A) I and II, I and III
    (B) I and IV, II and IV
    (C) II and III, II and IV
    (D) II and IV, III and IV
    (E) I and II, I and IV

14. Express $\sqrt{72}$ in simplest radical form.

    (A) $2\sqrt{18}$ (B) $3\sqrt{8}$ (C) $6\sqrt{2}$ (D) $5\sqrt{2}$ (E) $18\sqrt{2}$

15. If 15 students in a class average 80% on an English exam and 10 students average 90% on the same exam, what is the average in percent for all 25 students?
    (A) 86⅔%   (B) 85%   (C) 84%   (D) 83½%   (E) 83%

16. Find the tenth term of the series 5, 9, 14, 20, 27 . . .
    (A) 65   (B) 69   (C) 73   (D) 77   (E) 80

17. If the angles of a triangle are in the ratio 3:4:5, find the measure in degrees of the largest angle of the triangle.
    (A) 45   (B) 50   (C) 60   (D) 75   (E) 120

Quantitative Comparison

DIRECTIONS

In this section you will be given two quantities, one in column A and one in column B. You are to determine a relationship between the two quantities and mark—
    (A) if the quantity in column A is greater than the quantity in column B.
    (B) if the quantity in column B is greater than the quantity in column A.
    (C) if the quantities are equal.
    (D) if the comparison cannot be determined from the information that is given.

Column A   Column B

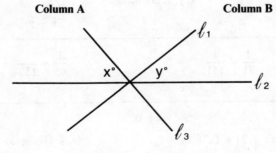

18.   x   y

_____

                        $a \neq 3$

19. $\dfrac{8}{a-3} + \dfrac{5}{3-a} - \dfrac{3}{a-3}$ 0

_____

	Column A	**Column B**
20.	Area of rectangle with length 8	Area of rectangle with width 7
21.	$\frac{1}{7}$	12%

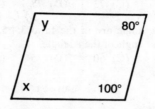

The figure is a parallelogram.

	Column A	**Column B**
22.	x	y

$$0 < x + y < 2$$

23.	x	y

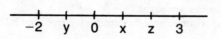

x, y, z, are integers

24.	z − x	x − y
25.	$\frac{1}{71} - \frac{1}{151}$	$\frac{1}{65} - \frac{1}{153}$

$$x > 0$$

26.	x(x + 2) + (x + 2)	(x + 1)(x + 3)
27.	Number of prime numbers between 3 and 19	5
28.	$\frac{1}{5} \times \frac{1}{3} \times \frac{4}{9}$	$\frac{1}{4} \times \frac{1}{2} \times \frac{5}{9}$

Column A	Column B

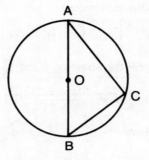

AB is a diameter

29.	∠ACB	∠CAB + ∠ABC

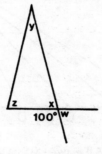

∠z = ∠w

30.	∠y + ∠x	100° + ∠z

x < y < z

31.	x + y + z	xyz

32.	Number of square inches in 1 square yard	Number of centimeters in 12.96 meters

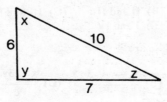

33.	∠y	∠x + ∠z

Solve each of the remaining problems in this section and blacken the corresponding space on the answer sheet.

34. If $x = -2$, then $x^3 - x^2 - x - 1 =$
    (A) 13   (B) 0   (C) -3 (D) -11 (E) -15

35. What is the average of the integers x, y, and z, if $x > z$ and $y < x$?

    (A) $\dfrac{x + z}{2}$ (B) y   (C) $\dfrac{2x + z}{3}$ (D) $\dfrac{x + y + z}{x + z}$

    (E) None of the above.

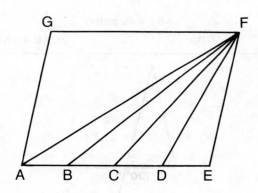

36. In the parallelogram, if $AB = BC = CD = DE$, then what is the ratio of the area of triangle CDF to the area of triangle ABF?
    (A) 4:1   (B) 2:1   (C) 1:1   (D) 1:4
    (E) Cannot be determined.

37. Which of the following terms has equal remainders?

    I. $\dfrac{4x - 6}{2}$ II. $\dfrac{6x + 8}{3}$ III. $\dfrac{8x + 10}{8}$ IV. $\dfrac{7x + 2}{2}$

    (A) I and II   (B) II and III   (C) III and IV
    (D) II and IV   (E) I and IV

38. If $x = y(3 + bc)$, then $b =$

    (A) $\dfrac{x + 3y}{cy}$ (B) $\dfrac{x - y - 3}{c}$ (C) $\dfrac{x - 3yc}{c}$

    (D) $\dfrac{x + 3yc}{c}$ (E) $\dfrac{x - 3y}{cy}$

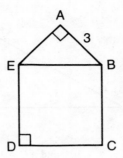

39. The figure is composed of a square and an isosceles right triangle. What is the perimeter of the figure?
    (A) 15   (B) $6 + 12\sqrt{2}$ (C) $6 + 3\sqrt{2}$ (D) 18
    (E) $6 + 9\sqrt{2}$

40. If $2/x = 4$ and if $2/y = 8$, then $x - y =$
    (A) ⅛   (B) ¼   (C) ¾   (D) 4   (E) 24

41. On a map, 1 centimeter represents 35 kilometers. Two cities 245 kilometers apart would be separated on the map by how many centimeters?
    (A) 5   (B) 7   (C) 9   (D) 210   (E) 280

42. A square has a diagonal 12 inches in length. What is the area of the square in square inches?
    (A) 24   (B) 48   (C) 72   (D) 144
    (E) Cannot be determined.

43. Which is the least of the following?

    (A) $\sqrt{5}$ (B) $\dfrac{5}{\sqrt{5}}$ (C) $\dfrac{\sqrt{5}}{5}$ (D) $\dfrac{1}{\sqrt{5}}$ (E) $\dfrac{1}{5}$

44. How many feet will an automobile travel in one second if it is moving at the rate of 30 miles per hour?
    (A) 44   (B) 66   (C) 88   (D) 176   (E) 2640

45. Bob can paint a house in 5 days and Fred can paint the same house in 6 days. How many days would it take to paint the house if they work together?
    (A) 1   (B) 2⁸⁄₁₁   (C) 3²⁄₉   (D) 4   (E) 5½

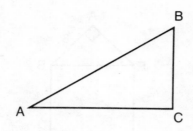

46. In △ABC, AC ⊥ BC, ∠A = 30°, and AC = 15. Find AB.
   (A) 22.5   (D) 11√2
   (B) 10√3   (E) Cannot be determined.
   (C) 30

47. Which of the following is an equation of a straight line parallel to the x-axis and passing through the point (4, −5)?
   (A) x = 4   (D) y = 4
   (B) y = −5   (E) cannot be determined
   (C) x = −5

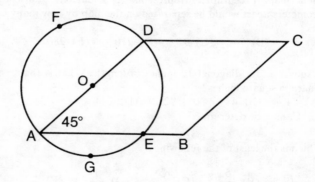

48. In the rhombus, BC ≃ 6, AE ≃ 4, and angle DAE ≃ 45°. AD is the diameter of the circle. If a man started at C and followed around the outer edge of this figure to D, F, A, G, E, B, and back to C, approximately how far did he travel?
   (A) 12 + 6π   (D) 14 + 6π
   (B) 14 + 27/4π   (E) 12 + 9/2π
   (C) 14 + 9/2π

49. A bus leaves Burbank at 9 A.M., traveling east at 50 miles per hour. At 1 P.M. a planes leaves Burbank traveling east at 300 miles per hour. At what time will the plane overtake the bus?

(A) 12:45 P.M.   (D) 1:48 P.M.
(B) 1:10 P.M.   (E) 1:55 P.M.
(C) 1:40 P.M.

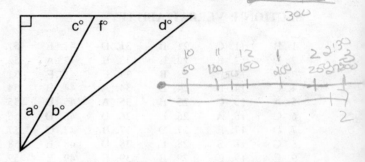

50. In the right triangle, c = 2a and d > 2b; therefore which of the following must be true?

(A) c > b + d
(B) angle a is greater than angle b
(C) angle a equals angle b
(D) angle b is greater than angle a
(E) angle d equals twice angle a

ANSWER KEY FOR THE PRACTICE TEST

The Mathematical Ability section in this Answer Key is coded so that you can quickly determine the math area in which you may need to concentrate your study time. AR = arithmetic, AL = algebra, and G = geometry.

SECTION I: VERBAL ABILITY

1. B	11. C	21. B	31. D	41. E	51. C	61. C
2. D	12. B	22. E	32. B	42. A	52. C	62. D
3. D	13. E	23. B	33. E	43. E	53. A	63. D
4. C	14. B	24. D	34. A	44. B	54. B	64. B
5. A	15. C	25. E	35. A	45. B	55. C	65. E
6. C	16. A	26. E	36. D	46. D	56. A	
7. D	17. E	27. D	37. B	47. C	57. B	
8. C	18. B	28. E	38. D	48. E	58. E	
9. E	19. C	29. B	39. E	49. B	59. E	
10. D	20. B	30. A	40. D	50. E	60. D	

SECTION II: MATHEMATICAL ABILITY

1. C (AL)	11. B (AL)	21. A (AR)	31. D (AL)	41. B (AR)
2. C (AR)	12. D (AR)	22. B (G)	32. C (AR)	42. C (G)
3. C (G)	13. B (AR)	23. D (AL)	33. A (G)	43. E (AR)
4. E (G)	14. C (AR)	24. B (AL)	34. D (AL)	44. A (AR)
5. B (AL)	15. C (AR)	25. B (AR)	35. E (AL)	45. B (AR)
6. D (G)	16. D (AR)	26. B (AL)	36. C (G)	46. B (G)
7. B (AR)	17. D (G)	27. C (AR)	37. B (AL)	47. B (AL)
8. C (AR)	18. D (G)	28. B (AR)	38. E (AL)	48. C (G)
9. E (AR)	19. C (AL)	29. C (G)	39. E (G)	49. D (AR)
10. B (G)	20. D (G)	30. B (G)	40. B (AL)	50. B (G)

HOW TO SCORE YOUR EXAM

1. Add the total number of correct responses for each Verbal Section.
2. Add the total number of incorrect responses (only those attempted or marked in) for each Verbal Section.
3. The total number of incorrect responses should be divided by 4, giving the adjustment factor.
4. Subtract this adjustment factor from the total number of correct responses to obtain a raw score in the Verbal Section.
5. This score is then scaled from 20 to 80.
6. Repeat this process for the Mathematical Section, but remember to divide the total of the incorrect QUANTITATIVE COMPARISON responses by 3, instead of 4.
7. The Mathematical Ability Raw Score is then scaled from 20 to 80.

Example:
A. If the total number of correct answers was 30 out of a possible 65.
B. And 20 problems were attempted but missed.
C. Dividing the 20 by 4 gives an adjustment factor of 5.
D. Subtracting this adjustment factor of 5 from the original 30 correct gives a raw score of 25.
E. This raw score is then scaled to the range of 20 to 80.

ANALYZING YOUR TEST RESULTS

The charts on the following pages should be used to carefully analyze your results and spot your strengths and weaknesses. The complete process of analyzing each subject area and each individual problem should be completed for each Practice Test. These results should then be reexamined for trends in types of errors (repeated errors) or poor results in specific subject areas. THIS REEXAMINATION AND ANALYSIS IS OF TREMENDOUS IMPORTANCE TO YOU IN ASSURING MAXIMUM TEST PREPARATION BENEFIT.

PRACTICE TEST: VERBAL ABILITY ANALYSIS SHEET

SECTION I: VERBAL ABILITY

	Possible	Completed	Right	Wrong
Antonyms	15			
Analogies	15			
Sentence Completion	15			
Reading Comprehension	20			
OVERALL VERBAL ABILITY TOTALS	65			

RAW SCORE = NUMBER RIGHT MINUS ONE-FOURTH POINT FOR EACH ONE
ATTEMPTED BUT MISSED. (NO POINTS SUBTRACTED FOR BLANK ANSWERS.)

PRACTICE TEST: MATHEMATICAL ABILITY ANALYSIS SHEET

SECTION II: MATHEMATICAL ABILITY

Math Ability	Possible	Completed	Right	Wrong
Arithmetic	14			
Algebra	9			
Geometry	11			
MATH ABILITY SUBTOTAL	(34)			

Quantitative Comparison	Possible	Completed	Right	Wrong
Arithmetic	5			
Algebra	5			
Geometry	6			
QUANTITATIVE COMPARISON SUBTOTAL	(16)			

OVERALL MATHEMATICAL ABILITY TOTALS	50			

RAW SCORE = NUMBER RIGHT MINUS ONE-FOURTH POINT FOR EACH ONE
ATTEMPTED BUT MISSED. (NO POINTS SUBTRACTED FOR BLANK ANSWERS.)

WHY??

ANALYSIS: TALLY SHEET FOR PROBLEMS MISSED

One of the most important parts of test preparation is analyzing WHY! you missed a problem so that you can reduce the number of mistakes. Now that you have taken the practice test and corrected your answers, carefully tally your mistakes by marking them in the proper column.

REASON FOR MISTAKE

	Total Missed	Simple Mistake	Misread Problem	Lack of Knowledge
SECTION I: VERBAL ABILITY				
SECTION II: MATH ABILITY				
TOTAL MATH AND VERBAL				

Reviewing the above data should help you determine WHY you are missing certain problems. Now that you have pinpointed the type of error, focus on avoiding your most common type.

COMPLETE ANSWERS AND EXPLANATIONS FOR PRACTICE TEST

SECTION I: VERBAL ABILITY

Antonyms

1. (B) Someone who is *humane* has the best qualities of mankind: kindness, tenderness, mercifulness. The opposite is *barbarous,* describing someone who is cruel, revolting, brutal, and uncivilized. "Terrible" means causing terror, and therefore is only a partial opposite of humane.

2. (D) *Bellicose* (*bell* = war) means inclined to fighting, hostile, quarrelsome. Its opposite, then, is *peaceful.* "Calm" is not correct because a calm person is not necessarily a non-hostile person.

3. (D) *Ineffable* (*in* = not; *fab* = to speak) describes something which is inexpressible or indescribable. Its opposite is *definable,* which means capable of being described exactly. "Cogent" refers to something which is convincingly to the point.

4. (C) *Repulsive* (*pel* = to push, to drive) refers to something which causes a strong dislike, something you want to push away. Its opposite is *attractive* (*tact* = to draw, to pull), which refers to something which draws positive reactions, which "pulls" you toward it.

5. (A) A *fable* (*fab* = to speak) is a fictitious story, often about animals, which teaches a moral lesson. The opposite here is *fact.*

6. (C) To *deport* (*port* = to carry) is to carry away or expel a person from a country. The opposite here is *welcome.*

7. (D) A *matriarch* (*arch* = the first, the leader) is a mother or the *female* ruler of a family or tribe. A *patriarch,* is the father or *male* ruler of a family or tribe.

8. (C) *Credulous* (*cred* = to believe) means easily convinced. The opposite is *unconvinceable.*

9. (E) *Poetical* describes a composition in verse, or any imaginative treatment of an unusual experience. *Prosaic* describes a composition not in verse, or that which is unimaginative, dull, and commonplace.

10. (D) A *proselyte* is one who has been convinced to adopt a new religion, political party, or opinion. An *apostate* (*apo* = from; *sta* = stand) is one who forsakes his former system of beliefs. A "renegade" is the deserter from an army or tribe; since a renegade does not necessarily desert beliefs, the word is not a near opposite of *proselyte.*

Analogies

11. (C) *Mountain* is to *peak* in the same way as *building* is to *roof*. The relationship here is one in which the highest part of a thing is compared to the thing itself. The best choice is (C), *building: roof,* as a roof is the highest part of a building in the same way a peak is the highest part of a mountain. In choice (B), "hill: ridge," a ridge is not necessarily the highest part of a hill.

12. (B) *Geometry* is to *triangle* in the same way as *botany* is to *daisy*. The relationship expressed here is a broad category compared to a narrow category within it. The best choice is (B), *botany: daisy,* as botany is a broad category encompassing the narrow category of daisy in the same way geometry encompasses triangle. In choice (A), "circle" is not as general a category as "shape," making it an incorrect choice. The same is true for choice (C), "teacher: education." Again, the narrow category precedes the general category, unlike *geometry: triangle,* in which the general category precedes the narrow.

13. (E) *Obvious* is to *evident* in the same way *allowed* is to *granted*. The relationship here is one of synonymous words. The best choice in this case is (E). These words are synonyms of each other as are *obvious* and *evident*. In choice (B), "fraudulent" is not a synonym of "funny." The word "funny" implies humor, while the word "fraudulent" implies deception, which may be either humorous or serious.

14. (B) *Dry* is to *parched* in the same way *wet* is to *soaked*. This involves a relationship of lesser degree to greater degree. In choice (A), the words "dishonest" and "crooked" are synonyms with equal implications of degree. The best choice is (B), *wet: soaked.*

15. (C) *Digit* is to *hand* in the same way as *key* is to *typewriter*. A *digit* is an essential part of a *hand* as a *key* is an essential part of a *typewriter*. In choice (A), both "skeleton" and "pancreas" are parts of the body system but are not parts of each other. In choice (B), "plateau" and "mountains" likewise are not parts of each other. Choice (D) also would not be appropriate, as "railroad" is a larger unit than "junction," reversing the sequence we find in *digit: hand,* where the first word, *digit,* is the smaller unit. Thus, the best choice is (C) *key: typewriter.*

16. (A) *Poor man* is to *slum* in the same way as *ship* is to *water*. In this relationship we present an element and its medium. The best choice is (A), *ship: water*. A poor man would probably be found in a slum, as in a similar fashion a ship would be found in water. In choice (C), the word "placebo" describes an element or effect used in many fields; (C) also lacks the specific relationship described in *poor man: slum.*

17. (E) *Car* is to *ignition* in the same way as *light* is to *switch*. The analogy here is one in which an object is made to function by the use of a second object. The best answer is (E) *light: switch,* as a *car* is turned on by an *ignition* in the same way a switch turns on a light.

18. (B) *Bestial* is to *brutish* in the same way as *frivolous* is to *trivial*. The relationship here is one of synonymous words. The best choice is (B), *frivolous: trivial*. In choice (D), "smirking" has a different connotation than "smiling."

19. (C) *Edifying* is to *enlightening* in the same way as *instructing* is to *teaching*. The relationship here is one of synonymous words, with the best choice being (C), *instructing: teaching*.

20. (B) *Monotheism* is to *theism* in the same way as *unicycle* is to *cycle*. *Monotheism* means belief in one God as opposed to *theism,* which is a more general term referring to belief in God or gods. The relationship here is from a specific singular belief to a more general belief. *Unicycle* is a specific type of one-wheeled cycle as opposed to the more general group of *cycles*. (E) is close, but "glasses" have only two complete lenses and therefore is not as general.

Sentence Completion

21. The correct answer is (B). Those who are "uncritical" of "regulation" would tend to hold *conventional* values. Along with this, *subsidization* (support) makes good sense.

22. The correct answer is (E), *symmetrical*. Since the arms or rays arise from a central portion, they would most likely be radially symmetrical. The only other possibility is choice (D), "rectangular," but this conflicts with "radially" and "arising from a central portion."

23. The best choice is (B), *potential*. The clue words in this sentence are "ratio" and "resistance." The word "resistance" has a negative connotation. "Ratio" suggests that the answer will need to contrast with "resistance." The only positive words provided as choices are (B), "potential," and (C), "excitement." Excitement does not provide the sentence with proper contextual meaning.

24. The best choice is (D), *consequently*. The semicolon is needed to connect the two clauses. The second part of the sentence positively extends the quality of the novel stated in the first part. The connecting word *consequently* provides the direction needed to extend the meaning of the first part of the sentence.

25. The best choice is (E), *comparing . . . expectations*. The signal clues are "unknown world" and "careful to note." "Careful to note" suggests careful thought or *comparing*, while "unknown world" suggests a meaning in this sentence that is best fulfilled by the word *expectations*. In choice (B), the word "refuting" is negative and does not convey the intended meaning of "careful to note."

26. The best choice is (E), *skeptical*. This is the only word which continues the negative message of the sentence without clashing with the context.

27. The best choice is (D), *indecisive*. It is the only choice that fits contextually and structurally into the sentence.

28. The best choice is (E), *vitiated . . . dilatory*. This choice conveys the negative meanings required by the sentence without clashing with its structure. *Vitiate* means to diminish the force or effectiveness of something, "to impair"; *dilatory* means characterized by procrastination, tending to delay.

29. The best choice is (B), *deprecate*. The phrase "Due to their bitter rivalry . . . " sets the tone for a negative choice. Choice (D), "thwart" is inappropriate, as the conclusions have already been reached and cannot, therefore, be "thwarted."

30. The best choice is (A), *palatial . . . sequester*. The phrase "from the rigors" requires that the second word in our choice convey a meaning of escape or hiding. The words "large" and "home" require a positive word that describes a home. Choice (A) is the only choice which meets these requirements.

Reading Comprehension

31. (D) Although the paragraph compares the sunset to a death, it simply and explicitly states, "the sun sank low." If anything is responsible for this imagined "death," it is the "gloom" which surrounds the big town in the west.

32. (B) The five men are the Director of Companies (captain), the Lawyer, the Accountant, Marlow, and the narrator.

33. (E) "The bones" seems to refer to something just mentioned, and it is *dominoes* that were just mentioned.

34. (A) In paragraph 4 the author says, "Between us there was . . . the bond of the sea."

35. (A) The first sentence tells us that the *Nellie* "was at rest."

36. (D) As the paragraph states, "genes are not directly observable."

37. (B) Environmental forces, such as cold, may affect the phenotype (paragraph 2). An interaction between the environment and the genotype results in the phenotype.

38. (D) Both phenotype and traits are mentioned as responses to the environment. The other choices are only indirectly related to phenotype.

39. (E) Anthropology is the only life science listed. It is the science that studies mankind in all its aspects, and therefore would include the information in the passage.

40. (D) Choices (A), (B), and (C) are all necessary results of a high U.S. GNP. But, as paragraph 3 states, the GNP does not measure "productive but unpaid work" such as keeping house; so a lower European GNP tells us nothing about how their households are maintained.

41. (E) Since the GNP measures material growth, an alternative type of growth would be non-material growth, of which spiritual growth is one type.

42. (A) In a fifth paragraph the author states, "Growth of the GNP has its costs," but without emphasizing those costs he soon concludes that "while . . . the social cost of a rising GNP seem[s] too high, it is likely that we would still be concerned about the growth of our nation's GNP." In other words, he deemphasizes the negative affects of a growing GNP in order to emphasize people's general appreciation of such growth. (B), (C), (D), and (E) are simply not true according to the passage.

43. (E) The second paragraph says that "the value of a product is what purchasers pay for it." The other factors which may help determine value are not listed as choices.

44. (B) Choices (A), (C), (D), and (E) are all listed as growth factors in the passage (paragraphs 6–8).

45. (B) Only answers B, D, and E could refer to *size*. (B) summarizes the information of paragraph 2, which tells us that an Eskimo's vocabulary is over 10,000 words, whereas the conversation between Eskimos and whites is made up of 300 to 600 words—less than one-tenth of the real Eskimo vocabulary.

46. (D) "Stefansson, the explorer," makes an observation about the Eskimo language in the second paragraph.

47. (C) The passage says that language "is the most traditional of

scholastic subjects." The only choice directly involving language is (C). And all of the other choices are very untraditional.

48. (E) This is directly stated in paragraph 2.

49. (B) Choice (E) contradicts the passage's extensive concentration on primitive language. (D) contradicts paragraph 2, where pidgin English is compared to a kind of Eskimo jargon different from native Eskimo. (C) and (A) each contain an unnecessary repetition: *primitive* and *old* are repetitious in (C); *complex* and *complicated* are repetitious in (A).

50. (E) Inflections are changes in the form and meaning of a word by adding prefixes and suffixes or merely changing the structure. (A) is too specific, while (B), (C), and (D) are clearly wrong by the passage.

51. (C) *Supplication* (*supple* = flexible; *pli* = to bend) is a humble request, often delivered on *bended knee*. The most nearly opposite action of a supplication, which *asks*, is a grant, which *gives*.

52. (C) *Redeem* (*re* = back; *empt, emere* = to buy, to take) means to set free by paying a ransom, or to buy back. Its opposite is *imprison*, to take freedom away. "Condemn," an almost-opposite, may have to do with inflicting a penalty, but does not clearly connote loss of freedom.

53. (A) *Prudence* is good judgment. Its opposite is *folly* (foolishness).

54. (B) To *distend* (*tend* = to stretch) is to swell or become inflated. The opposite is *deflate*.

55. (C) *Luxuriant* (*lux* = extravagance) means plentiful and is usually used to describe something which is abundant in growth. The opposite is small. "Miserly" is also opposite to plentiful, but since it refers to hoarding money, it is more nearly opposite to the idea of abundant wealth, not abundant growth.

56. (A) *Opaque* is to *clear* in the same way as *authentic* is to *false*. The relationship here is one of two adjectives which are antonyms. The best choice is (A) *authentic: false*.

57. (B) *Tiger* is to *carnivore* in the same way as *train* is to *vehicle*. The relationship expressed here is a narrow category compared to a broad category. The best choice in this case is (B), *train: vehicle*, since train falls into the category of vehicle in the same way a *tiger* is a *carnivore*. Choice (A) is inappropriate, since stove does not fall into the category of kitchen, although it may be a part of a kitchen. Choice (D) is also inappropriate, as

parakeet and parrot are two different kinds of birds that happen to be related.

58. (E) *Jaunty* is to *perky* in the same way as *par* is to *equal*. The relationship here is one of synonymous words. *Jaunty* and *perky* are synonyms, as are *par* and *equal*. None of the other choices presents a set of synonyms. In choice (B) the word "caustic" has a bitter connotation which it does not share with the more neutral word, "witty." Thus, choice (B) does not present a set of synonyms. The best choice is (E) *par: equal*.

59. (E) *Ambiguous* is to *clear* in the same way as *indefinite* is to *definite*. The relationship here is one of opposites. *Ambiguous* means "unclear or indefinite." *Clear* means "specific or definite." *Indefinite* is the opposite of *definite*.

60. (D) *Anarchy* is to *uncontrolled* in the same way as *oligarchy* is to *controlled*. The relationship here is one of governmental philosophy and a typical quality of that philosophy. *Anarchy,* a state of lawlessness, is typically *uncontrolled*. *Oligarchy,* government by a select few, is typically *controlled*.

61. The best choice is (C), *malaise . . . harrowing*. The word "lowered" requires that both words in our choice be negative. The word "productivity" requires that the first word in our choice describe "workers' " attitudes affecting productivity. Looking at our choices, the first word would have to be *malaise*.

62. The best choice is (D), *fathom* (comprehend). It is the only choice fitting the context of the sentence.

63. The best choice is (D), *fail . . . operational*. The signal here is "cannot _____ to be impressed," which should be a negative word, while the second choice should be a complement to "structural," which is *operational*.

64. The best choice is (B), *fabricate . . . unbelievable*. Choice (A) is a valid possibility. It is not the best choice, however, as "foolhardy" generally refers to an action. The word "story" fits better contextually and structurally in this sentence with the word *unbelievable*.

65. The best choice is (E), *experienced . . . organs*. This choice offers clarity to the sentence. Choice (C) is a possibility, but the word "felt" poorly defines the actions needed to describe what the words "Our senses . . . " do. Our seeing, hearing, and other senses all experience. It is generally agreed upon that the only sense where we are certain to feel is the sense of touch.

SECTION II: MATHEMATICAL ABILITY

1. (C) Dividing the original equation by 3, gives

$$\frac{3x}{3} + \frac{6y}{3} = \frac{21}{3},$$

   or $x + 2y = 7$.

2. (C) Since $1\frac{1}{5} = \frac{6}{5}$ its reciprocal is $\frac{5}{6}$

   Hence the sum of $1\frac{1}{5} + \frac{5}{6} = \frac{6}{5} + \frac{5}{6}$

$$= \frac{36}{30} + \frac{25}{30}$$

$$= \frac{61}{30}$$

$$= 2\frac{1}{30}$$

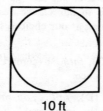

10 ft

3. (C) Since the diameter of the circle equals the side of the square, then the diameter equals 10. The radius is then 5. Using the formula,

   area of circle $= \pi r^2$
   $= \pi(5)^2$
   $= 25\pi$ square feet.

4. (E) Since there are 360° in a circle (clock in this case), then going around twice gives 720°. From 12 o'clock to 3 o'clock is another 90°, totaling 810°.

5. (B) If m + 5 is an even integer, than m must be an odd integer because an odd integer added to another odd integer gives an even integer. Hence m is the only choice which is not an even integer.

6. (D) Charting Tom's trip would look like this:

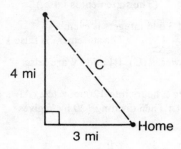

Since the directions are west and north, we have a right angle, allowing us to use the Pythagorean theorem to find the length of the third side of the triangle (which is Tom's actual distance from home).

$$a^2 + b^2 = c^2$$
$$3^2 + 4^2 = c^2$$
$$9 + 16 = c^2$$
$$25 = c^2$$
$$5 = c$$

Therefore, the correct answer is (D). Tom's actual distance from home is 5 miles. (You may have noticed the 3:4:5 common right triangle relationship and avoided using the Pythagorean theorem).

7. (B) Multiply both numerator and denominator by 12 (the lowest common denominator):

$$\frac{12 \quad (1/2 + 1/3 + 1/4)}{12 \quad (1/4 + 1/6 + 1/12)} = \frac{6 + 4 + 3}{3 + 2 + 1}$$

$$= \frac{13}{6}$$

$$= 2\frac{1}{6}$$

8. (C) If you are unfamiliar with the rules, try simple numbers for each situation that will make them false.

  I. The sum of 2 even integers is even.
    $2 + 2 = 4$ $4 + 4 = 8$ (always true)

  II. The product of 2 even integers is even.
    $4 \times 2 = 8$ $2 \times 8 = 16$ (always true)

III. The sum of 2 odd integers is odd.

$3 + 3 = 6$ (The statement is false.)

IV. The sum of 3 odd integers is even.

$3 + 5 + 7 = 15$ (The statement is false.)

The correct answer is (C), III and IV are false.

9. (E) First change 2 hours into 120 minutes. (Always get a common unit of measurement.) Then dividing 120 by $\frac{2}{3}$ gives

$$\overset{60}{\cancel{120}} \times \frac{3}{\cancel{2}} = 180.$$

The correct answer is (D), 180 items. Notice choices (A) and (B) are ridiculous answers.

10. (B) The area of $\triangle MNP = \frac{1}{2} bh = \frac{1}{2} (MN)(MP)$.
Since $\triangle MNP$ is a right triangle, the Pythagorean theorem says

$$c^2 = a^2 + b^2$$
$$(NP)^2 = (MP)^2 + (MN)^2$$
$$26^2 = 24^2 + (MN)^2$$
$$676 = 576 + (MN)^2$$
$$(MN)^2 = 100$$
$$MN = \sqrt{100} = 10$$

Hence the area of $\triangle MNP = \frac{1}{2} (MN)(MP)$
$$= \frac{1}{2} (10)(24)$$
$$= 120$$

11. (B) This problem is most easily solved by working from the answers. Divide each of the answers by 5 and notice that choice (A) is eliminated, since it does not give a remainder of 1.

$$\frac{12}{5} = 2r2; \quad \frac{16}{5} = 3r1; \quad \frac{21}{5} = 4r1; \quad \frac{6}{5} = 1r1; \quad \frac{11}{5} = 2r1$$

Now dividing the remaining choices by 3 gives

$$\frac{16}{3} = 5r1; \quad \frac{21}{3} = 7; \quad \frac{6}{3} = 2; \quad \frac{11}{3} = 3r2$$

The correct choice is (E), 11, which when divided by 5 has a remainder of 1 and when divided by 3 has a remainder of 2.

12. (D) Simplify the expression as follows:

$$\frac{\left(\frac{2}{3}\right)^2 - 3}{2 - (.5)^2} = \frac{\frac{4}{9} - 3}{2 - .25}$$

$$\frac{-2\frac{5}{9}}{1.75} = \frac{-\frac{23}{9}}{1\frac{3}{4}} = \frac{\frac{-23}{9}}{\frac{7}{4}} = \frac{-23}{9} \times \frac{4}{7} = -\frac{92}{63}$$

The correct answer is (D).

13. (B) Checking each possible pair of numbers for common divisions:

I.   3⎱Only common divisor 1;
II. 4⎰these are relatively prime.

I.   3⎱Only common divisor 1;
III. 7⎰these are relatively prime.

I.   3⎱Common divisors are 1 and 3;
IV. 12⎰these are NOT relatively prime.

Since I and IV are NOT relatively prime, check the choices to see which include I and IV. Notice that I and IV are only in choices (B) and (E); therefore those are the two possible choices. A closer look eliminates choice (E) because I and II have numbers that are relatively prime. For good measure, checking II and IV:

II.   4⎱Common divisors are 1 and 4.
IV. 12⎰These are NOT relatively prime.

Therefore I and IV, and II and IV are NOT relatively prime, giving the correct answer of (B).

14. (C) Factoring $\sqrt{72}$ gives $\sqrt{36 \times 2}$ or $\sqrt{36} \times \sqrt{2}$.

Since the square root of 36 is 6, simplified form is $6\sqrt{2}$.

15. (C) In this type of problem (weighted average) you must multiply the number of students times their respective scores and divide this total by the number of students as follows:

$$\begin{array}{r} 15 \times 80 = 1200 \\ \underline{10 \times 90 = 900} \\ 25 2100 \end{array}$$

Now divide 25 into 2100. This leaves an average of 84%, therefore the correct answer is (B).

16. (D) In the series 5, 9, 14, 20, 27 . . . we have

$$9 - 5 = 4$$
$$14 - 9 = 5$$
$$20 - 14 = 6$$
$$27 - 20 = 7$$

Hence the difference between the terms is increasing by 1 each time.

The sixth term would be $27 + 8 = 35$
The seventh term would be $35 + 9 = 44$
The eighth term would be $44 + 10 = 54$
The ninth term would be $54 + 11 = 65$
The tenth term would be $65 + 12 = 77$

17. (D) To solve:

Let $3x$ = 1st angle
     $4x$ = 2nd angle
     $5x$ = 3rd angle

Then $3x + 4x + 5x = 180$
$$12x = 180$$
$$x = 15$$
$$3x = 45$$
$$4x = 60$$
$$5x = 75$$

Hence the largest angle of the triangle has a measure of 75°.

Quantitative Comparison—Answers 18–33

18. (D) Since x and y are not vertical angles and no other information is given, no comparison can be made. The correct answer is (D).

19. (C) Simplifying the first column gives

$$\frac{8}{a - 3} + \frac{5}{3 - a} - \frac{3}{a - 3}$$

$$\frac{5}{a - 3} + \frac{5}{-1(a - 3)}$$

$$\frac{5}{a - 3} + \frac{-5}{a - 3} = 0$$

20. (D) Since two dimensions, length and width are necessary to find the area of a rectangle, and only one dimension is given in each case, then no comparison is possible. The correct answer is (D).

21. (A) Changing $\frac{1}{7}$ to a percent as follows is one method

$$\frac{1}{7} = \frac{x}{100} \qquad 100 = 7x \qquad x = \frac{100}{7} \qquad x = 12+$$

There is no need to calculate any further, as a comparison can now be made.

Alternate Method: Since $\frac{1}{8}$ is $12\frac{1}{2}\%$ and $\frac{1}{7}$ is greater than $\frac{1}{8}$, then $\frac{1}{7}$ is greater than 12%.

22. (B) In a parallelogram, opposite angles are equal, therefore x = 80° and y = 100°. The correct answer is (B) x < y.

23. (D) Substituting 0 for x and 1 for y fits the condition 0 < x + y < 2 (0 < 0 + 1 < 2) and gives an answer of (B), column B is greater. Now substituting 1 for x and 0 for y, also fits the condition 0 < x + y < 2 (0 < 1 + 0 < 2) but gives an answer of (A), column A is greater. Therefore the correct answer is (D), since different values give different comparisons, no comparison can be made.

24. (B) On the number line, if x, y, and z are integers, then by inspection x = 1, y = −1 and z = 2. Substituting these values into each column gives

$$2 - 1 \quad \text{and} \quad 1 - (-1)$$
hence $\qquad 1 \qquad < \qquad 2$

Therefore the correct answer is (B).

25. (B) Finding a common denominator is not necessary here. Make a partial comparison by comparing the first fraction in each column, 1/71 is smaller than 1/65. Now comparing the second fractions that are being subtracted, 1/151 is greater than 1/153. If you start with a smaller number and subtract a greater number, it must be less than starting with a greater number and subtracting a smaller one.

26. (B) Simplifying column A by using the distributing property, leaves

(x + 1)(x + 2) and (x + 1)(x + 3)
Canceling x + 1 from each side, leaves x + 2 and x + 3
(This can be done because x > 0).

Then canceling x from each side gives 2 and 3.

Therefore the correct answer is (B), $2 < 3$.

27. (C) The prime numbers between 3 and 19 are 5, 7, 11, 13, and 17. The correct answer is (C), since there are 5 primes.

28. (B) This problem is most easily answered by inspection. Notice that each fraction in column B is greater than the corresponding fraction in column A. Therefore multiplying the fractions is not necessary.

29. (C) Since triangle ACB is inscribed in a semicircle, angle C is 90°. Because there are 180° in a triangle, the sum of the remaining angles ∠CAB and ∠ABC must total 90°. Therefore the correct answer is (C).

30. (B) Angles x and w each equal 80° (a straight line contains 180°). Since ∠z = 80°, then ∠y = 20°. Therefore ∠y + ∠x = 100°. 100° + ∠z = 100° + 80° = 180°.

31. (D) Substituting 0 for x, 1 for y and 2 for z, gives

$(0) + (1) + (2)$ $(0)(1)(2)$
therefore $3 > 0$

Now substituting −1 for x, 0 for y and 1 for z gives

$(-1) + (0) + (1)$ $(-1)(0)(1)$
therefore $0 = 0$

Since different values give different comparisons, the correct answer is (D).

32. (C) Since there are 9 square feet in 1 square yard, and 144 square inches in 1 square foot, then $1 \times 9 \times 144 = 1296$ is the number of square inches in 1 square yard. Therefore column A is 1296. Since there are 100 centimeters in 1 meter, then $100 \times 12.96 = 1296$ is the number of centimeters in 12.96 meters. Therefore column B is also 1296, and the columns are equal.

33. (A) In a 3-4-5 triangle (or 6-8-10), the angle opposite the largest side equals 90°. Thus the sum of the other two angles also equals 90°. Notice, however, that this triangle is 6-7-10. Thus the angle opposite the "7" side is decreased slightly. Therefore, the sum of the two other angles will no longer equal 90°, so ∠y will be greater than the sum of ∠x and ∠z.

34. **(D)** Substituting:

If $x = -2$, $x^3 - x^2 - x - 1 = (-2)^3 - (-2)^2 - (-2) - 1$
$$= -8 - 4 + 2 - 1$$
$$= -12 + 2 - 1$$
$$= -10 - 1$$
$$= -11$$

Hence $x^3 - x^2 - 1 = -11$

35. **(E)** The average of the integers x, y, and z is $(x + y + z)/3$, regardless of which variables are greater. (Remember to find an average, total the numbers and divide the actual number of items.) Since $(x + y + z)/3$ is not given as a choice, the correct answer is **(E)**.

36. **(C)** In parallelogram AEFG if all of the triangles have the same base, and they all meet at F (giving them all the same height), since the formula for area of a triangle is $\frac{1}{2} \times$ base $\times$ height, then they all have equal areas. Therefore the ratio of the area of triangle CDF to the area of triangle ABF is 1:1 and the correct answer is **(B)**.

37. **(B)** Dividing out each term gives

I. $\dfrac{4x - 6}{2} = 2x - 3$ (no remainder)

II. $\dfrac{6x + 8}{3} = 2x + 2$, remainder 2

III. $\dfrac{8x + 10}{8} = x + 1$, remainder 2

IV. $\dfrac{7x + 2}{2} = 3x + 1$, remainder x

Since you are looking for equal remainders, the correct answer is **(B)**, II and III.

38. **(E)** Solve for b as follows:

$x = y(3 + bc)$
$x = 3y + bcy$
$x - 3y = bcy$
$\dfrac{x - 3y}{cy} = b$

39. (E) Since triangle ABE is isosceles, AB = AE, and each leg of the triangle is 3. Using the Pythagorean theorem gives

$$3^2 + 3^2 = BE^2$$
$$9 + 9 = BE^2$$
$$18 = BE^2$$
$$\sqrt{18} = BE$$

Simplifying $\sqrt{18} = \sqrt{9 \cdot 2} = 3\sqrt{2}$

$3\sqrt{2}$ is the length of the side of the square. Now totaling the outside sides of the square and the triangle $3 + 3 + 3\sqrt{2} + 3\sqrt{2} + 3\sqrt{2}$ leaves 6 $+ 9\sqrt{2}$. Therefore the correct answer is (E).

40. (B) Solving the first equation for x as follows:

$$\frac{2}{x} = 4$$

$$2 = 4x$$

$$\frac{2}{4} = x$$

therefore $\frac{1}{2} = x$

Now solving the second equation for y,

$$\frac{2}{y} = 8$$

$$2 = 8y$$

$$\frac{2}{8} = y$$

therefore $\frac{1}{4} = y$

Substituting these values for $x - y$ gives $\frac{1}{2} - \frac{1}{4} = \frac{2}{4} - \frac{1}{4} = \frac{1}{4}$

Therefore $x - y = \frac{1}{4}$, and the correct answer is (A).

41. (B) Solve by setting up a proportion:

If 1 cm = 35 km
then x cm = 245 km

and $\dfrac{1}{x} = \dfrac{35}{245}$

$35x = 245$

$\dfrac{35x}{35} = \dfrac{245}{35}$

$x = 7$

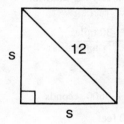

42. (C) Using the Pythagorean theorem and substituting gives

$a^2 + b^2 = c^2$

$s^2 + s^2 = 12^2$
$2s^2 = 144$
$s^2 = 72$
$s = \sqrt{72}$

Since area is s^2, then $(\sqrt{72})^2 = 72$

Alternate solution: Area of square = ½ × diagonal squared
= ½ × 12²
= 72

43. (E) Choices (A) and (B) can be eliminated immediately, as they are greater than 1 and (C), (D), and (E) are less than 1. Approximating, $\sqrt{5}$ = 2.2 gives

(C) $\dfrac{2.2}{5}$ (D) $\dfrac{1}{2.2}$ (E) $\dfrac{1}{5}$

(C) and (D) are close to ½, while (E) is obviously the smallest.

An alternate method would be to square each number as follows (this would magnify the difference).

(A) $(\sqrt{5})^2 = 5$

(B) $\left(\dfrac{5}{\sqrt{5}}\right)^2 = \dfrac{25}{5} = 5$

(C) $\left(\dfrac{\sqrt{5}}{5}\right)^2 = \dfrac{5}{25} = \dfrac{1}{5}$

(D) $\left(\dfrac{1}{\sqrt{5}}\right)^2 = \dfrac{1}{5}$

(E) $\left(\dfrac{1}{5}\right)^2 = \dfrac{1}{25}$

Choice (E) is again obviously the smallest.

44. (A) 30 miles per hour $= \dfrac{30 \text{ miles}}{1 \text{ hour}}$

Since 1 mile $= 5280$ feet

and 1 hour $= 60$ minutes $= 3600$ seconds

$$\frac{30 \text{ miles}}{1 \text{ hour}} = \frac{30 \times 5280 \text{ feet}}{1 \times 3600 \text{ seconds}}$$

$$= 44 \text{ feet per second}$$

Hence the automobile will travel 44 feet in one second.

45. (B) By inspecting the answers, (B) is the only reasonable choice. If Bob and Fred each worked at a rate of one house for every 6 days, then working together, they would be able to complete a house in 3 days. Since Bob works at a slightly faster rate, it would take slightly less than 3 days.

Mathematically,
Let x = number of days working together

Then $\dfrac{x}{5} + \dfrac{x}{6} = 1$

$30\left(\dfrac{x}{5} + \dfrac{x}{6}\right) = 1 \ (30)$

$6x + 5x = 30$

$11x = 30$

Therefore $x = {}^{30}\!/_{11}$, or $2{}^{8}\!/_{11}$

46. **(B)** In $\triangle ABC$, $\angle A = 30°$, $\angle C = 90°$, and $\angle B = 60°$,

Hence $AC = \dfrac{\sqrt{3}}{2}$ (AB),

$AC = 15 = \dfrac{\sqrt{3}}{2}$ (AB)

$AB = (15)\left(\dfrac{2}{\sqrt{3}}\right) = \dfrac{30}{\sqrt{3}} = \dfrac{30\sqrt{3}}{3} = 10\sqrt{3}$

47. **(B)** A line parallel to the x-axis and passing through $(4, -5)$ will also pass through all y's at -5. Thus $y = -5$.

Alternate Method: A line parallel to the x-axis has the general equation $y = c$, where c is some constant value of y.

Since $y = -5$ in the ordered pair $(4, -5)$, the equation of the line passing through this point and parallel to the x-axis must be $y = -5$.

48. **(C)** Since ABCD is a rhombus, all sides are equal; therefore BC = CD $\simeq$ 6 and BC + CD $\simeq$ 12. AB $\simeq$ 6, minus AE $\simeq$ 4, leaves $6 - 4 = 2$, which is the length of BE. Adding $12 + 2 = 14$, gives the distance around the rhombus that will be traveled. Now using the formula for circumference of a circle = $2\pi r$, or πD, leaves 6π as the circumference of the complete circle. Because the inscribed angle is 45°, arc DE is 90° (inscribed angle is half of the arc it intercepts). This 90° will not be traveled, as it is in the interior of the figure, therefore only 270° of the 360° in the complete circle will be traveled, or $\frac{3}{4}$ of the circle. $\frac{3}{4} \times 6\pi = 9\pi/2$. This added to the original 14 gives answer (C) $14 + 9\pi/2$.

49. **(D)** Set up the equation as follows: Let t be the length of time it will take the plane to overtake the bus, then $t + 4$ is the time that the bus has traveled before the plane starts. The distance that the bus has traveled by 1 P.M. is $50(t + 4)$, since distance equals rate times time $(d = rt)$. The distance the plane will travel is $300t$. Now equating these two (they will have to travel the same distance for one to overtake the other), gives $50(t + 4) = 300t$.

Solve the equation as follows:

$$50(t + 4) = 300t$$
$$50t + 200 = 300t$$
$$200 = 250t$$

therefore $\frac{4}{5} = t$

$\frac{4}{5}$ of an hour ($\frac{4}{5} \times 60$) is 48 minutes. Hence it will take 48 minutes for the plane to overtake the bus, and since the plane is starting at 1 P.M., it will overtake the bus at 1:48 P.M.

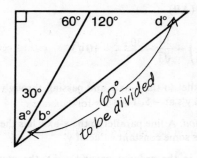

50. (B) In the right triangle, if c = 2a, then angle a = 30° and c = 60°. Since angle f is supplemetary to angle c, angle f must be 120°. If angle f is 120°, then there are 60° left to be divided between angles d and b (remember there are 180° in a triangle). Since d > 2b, then b must be less than 30°; therefore the correct answer is (B), angle a (30°) is greater than angle b (less than 30°).

Notice the way you should have marked the diagram to assist you.

FINAL PREPARATION: "The Final Touches"

1. Make sure that you are familiar with the testing center location and nearby parking facilities.

2. The last week of preparation should be spent primarily on reviewing strategies, techniques, and directions for each area.

3. Don't *cram* the night before the exam. It's a waste of time!

4. Remember to bring the proper materials to the test—identification, admission ticket, three or four sharpened Number 2 pencils, a watch, and a good eraser.

5. Start off crisply, working the ones you know first, and then coming back and trying the others.

6. If you can eliminate one or more of the choices, make an educated guess.

7. Mark in reading passages, underline key words, write out information, make notations on diagrams, take advantage of being permitted to write in the test booklet.

8. Make sure that you are answering "what is being asked" and that your answer is reasonable.

9. Using the Two Successful Overall Approaches (p. 7) is the key to getting the ones right that you should get right—resulting in a good score on the PSAT/NMSQT.

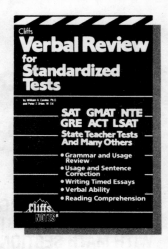